# Out of Wonder

## The Evolving Story of the Universe

**Nellie McLaughlin**

*VERITAS*

*First published* 2004 *by*
Veritas Publications
7/8 Lower Abbey Street
Dublin 1
Ireland
Email publications@veritas.ie
Website www.veritas.ie

10 9 8 7 6 5 4 3 2

ISBN 978 1 85390 648 0

Reprinted 2009

Verses from 'A Christmas Childhood', 'To A Child' and 'Poplar Memory', all
by Patrick Kavanagh, reprinted with the permission of the Trustees of the
Estate of the late Katherine B. Kavanagh, through the Jonathan Williams
Literary Agency. Verses from 'At Blackwater Pond' and 'The Sea' by Mary
Oliver (Beacon Press). Extract from 'Our Origins Are In The Sea' by Eavan
Boland, from *Outside History* (Carcanet, 1990).

*A catalogue record for this book is available from the British Library.*

Designed & Typeset by Paula Ryan.

Cover Art work by Oonagh Campbell, Sister of Mercy,
Northern Province, Ireland.

Oonagh experiences art-making as a process in which tiny glimpses of the
ancient and ever-present creative energy of the universe can be gleaned.

Printed in the Republic of Ireland by Colour Books Ltd, Dublin

*Veritas books are printed on paper made from the wood pulp of managed forests. For every tree
felled, at least one tree is planted, thereby renewing natural resources.*

To my parents, May and Thomas, and my brother Tom
whose memory lives on.

To my family, friends and Inishowen bioregion, who
together have gifted me with life, love, laughter,
imagination and faith as well as a lively sense of belonging
in the community of life.

# CONTENTS

# ACKNOWLEDGEMENTS

'If the only prayer you say in your whole life is 'thank you' that would suffice'

Meister Eckhart

I celebrate with thankfulness the gift of life, my ancestors, parents and present companions in the community of the Universe, who have inspired this publication.

I value the wisdom and vision of Thomas Berry and Brian Swimme, together with Miriam Therese MacGillis and her companions at Genesis farm, NJ, for introducing me to the new story of the Universe and for igniting my passion for living in harmony with the Earth.

I treasure the friendship of the North-West Genesis Group, Donegal who, through their love of nature, expertise, practical advice and technical support have made this book possible.

I rejoice with Oonagh Campbell in the beauty and vibrancy of her art, which graces the cover of *Out of Wonder: the Evolving Story of the Universe*.

I appreciate the insights, ideas, questions and challenges offered by so many participants at cosmology, ecology and sustainable living seminars and programmes over the past four years.

I am grateful to the Sisters of Mercy, Northern Province, for the opportunity to write this book and to many companions and friends, who have read and critically appraised it.

I cherish the understanding, support and encouragement of my family and the fun and sense of perspective created by the children – Simone, Aisling, Keith, Chloe and Caleb.

I thank Maura Hyland, Director, Veritas Publications, for inviting me to write this book and to the staff of Veritas, especially Helen Carr, Toner Quinn and Paula Ryan for their expert advice and encouragement.

# FOREWORD

Memories echo the enduring moments of life. I remember the first time I prepared onions for Irish stew. It was my first year in secondary school and we were learning to cook, by the book, as it were. That attempt ended in tears, as has every single one since then. Onions are bulbous root vegetables with many protective layers. Peeling one's way to the silky white core is a tearful process. However, the memory of tears soon evaporates in the aroma and flavour of the resultant meal. I like to think of an onion as an image of the universe. The awesome story of the universe has its roots in the flaring forth moment of the original fireball over thirteen billion years ago. Stars, rocks, water, plants, insects, birds, animals and humans sing the memory of the great cosmos simply by being as they are. My ancestral memory courses through my veins, crystallises my bones and broadens my smile while guiding my every movement. We have so many layers to unravel in order to get in touch with our deepest roots, not merely millions of years but billions!

*Out of Wonder: The Evolving Story of the Universe* is a journey. It is a trip down memory lane to the heart of the universe and the great unfolding of energy, of life and consciousness. At the same time it is an engagement with my own story, a journey to my inner depths, a profound encounter with life in its evolutionary and mystical wonder. Like the onion, our story is multi-layered, a series of intertwining stories creating our cosmic identity. The story of stars and galaxies, the story of Earth in all its life forms and the human story are one. This is the magnificent outpouring of divine creativity embracing the radical unity of all life. All species are different but not separate in the wonder of creation. Getting in touch with this oneness can be painful as we try to prise fixed mindsets. It hurts to expand our story to include all of life, non-human as well as human, and it certainly pains us to acknowledge that we are not alone as the epitome of God's creative genius. We feel the muscle stretch in loosening the memories of almost fourteen billion years. What a painful but invigorating jolt from the restricting confines of so-called recorded history. The thirteen billion year story is recorded in the rocks, the stars, in the soil, in water and in the fibre of every being.

Like the onion shedding its tightly fitting layers, we too are challenged to be more open to the gradual unfolding of the story of life within the great cosmic weaving. The unique flavour of the onion is not lost in the mix; rather it contributes its own particular flavour to the whole and enhances it. As we expand our identity as humans to embrace every other life form, each a unique manifestation of divine art, what will emerge? An overwhelming sense of the oneness of all life will transform us. Our uniqueness and the uniqueness of every being will merge, opening us to the wonder of life and who we are as species among species in the community we call the universe.

This book is structured around the emergence of life in its unity and diversity with three identifiable movements. The first is the story of the universe. We will listen in the first seven chapters to the universe speaking through the wonder of creation. This is our origin story as it is presently unfolding through the combined wisdom of generations in the community of life and with ever more powerful telescopes and microscopes. In the opening chapter *Out of Wonder,* we catch a glimpse of the variety, beauty, turbulence and mystery of creation and how it has baffled people from the beginning. Today with our advancing technologies we are no less astonished as we realise that the more we know the more there is to know. May we never cease to live out of wonder into delight. In *Out of Emptiness – Life in a Fireball,* we imagine the miracle moment and connect with the passion for creativity at the heart of the Universe. In that awesome moment when the stars were born and galaxies formed, the energy to direct the expansion of the Universe ever since was holding all of us potentially in deep space. May we delight in the abundance of life and richness emanating from the original fireball. *Out of Fire* takes us into the heat of possibility as we swirl in the vast expanses of space in the birthing of the Sun and solar system some five billion years ago. *Out of the Dance* begins with an invitation to imagine a time before rocks and water, forests and grass, a time before colour and fragrance, a world without birdsong, the buzz of insects or the vital presence of plants, flowers, animals and people. All that changed about 4.5 billion years ago with the birth of the Earth within the Solar System. The Earth, a privileged planet, slowed and cooled sufficiently to form an atmosphere, rock structure and oceans. Gradually and mysteriously the earliest life forms emerged within the oceans and earth danced into life. May the wisdom that inspired our ancestors of old to align their lives with the Sun and rhythms of Earth enable us to experience the radiance of harmony and delight in the oneness of all life.

*Out of the Waters* brings us to new depths of understanding as our eyes and hearts are washed clean of the grit and debris that cloud our vision in the contemplation of the extent and variety of the community with which we share the Universe. The Earth is alive! May we never cease to wonder and celebrate. In *Out of the Trees* we learn about our ancient forebears – the early hominids – who lived in the trees. When did we come down from the trees? What did it feel like to stand and stare, away from the forest canopies? Standing upright was a defining moment as we trace the emergence of the modern human. The human is the being in whom the Universe becomes self-consciously aware. Discovering fire, making tools, hunting and gathering, the emergence of language, song, dance, art and ritual characterise our early journeying. *Out of the Countryside* traces the roaming of our ancestors as they moved from the open spaces to settle in larger, more settled communities. River valleys, endowed with fertile soil and abundant water, were most popular and here great civilisations took shape: the Middle East, North Africa, China and India. What a rich tapestry was to emerge in terms of cultural, social, economic, political and religious life from the relentless flow of early settlements to the Neanderthals and indigenous peoples of the world. What were some of the gains and some of the losses over the millennia in terms of the total community of life?

The second movement of the book highlights the changing relations between the human and the natural world – a process accelerated by the Industrial Revolution of the seventeenth and eighteenth centuries. What are some of the changes being asked of us in light of the awesome story of the

Universe? What shifts of mind-set and behaviour do we need to make? One of the implications of the growing alienation between the human and natural world has been the dominant stance of the human and how we are upsetting the balance of nature, for example: biodiversity, water, soil, deforestation, waste management, global warming and climate change. The final chapter, *Out of Respect*, is a passionate plea to reconnect more deeply with the natural world and find our rightful place within it. This calls for a new humility in our lives. How might we live in a more mutually enhancing and sustaining way? The challenge is to shift from being *apart from* to being *part of* the community of all creation; this is our context. Drawing on the collective wisdom of all creation, especially the three guiding principles of the universe: *diversity, interiority and interconnectedness*, and the Earth as an alive, self-regulating and self-sustaining organism, I offer some possibilities around trying to live in this new consciousness of the oneness of all. What are some of the choices we need to make at this crucial time?

This book is inspired by the mystery of creation. I write from my own perspective as a Christian in the conviction that the universe story transcends all religions, nationalities cultures and traditions. The universe is all embracing; all belong in that great curvature of space and time. I am not a scientist, therefore, I tell the scientific story of the Universe in lay terms as well as from a more Irish and feminine perspective. In so doing I am keen to weave patterns of wisdom and enchantment from various ages and characters, circles of hope and delight in the magnificence of life, patterns of resources in the face of aggression and destruction to the very fabric of existence and cushions of comfort amid mounting losses in the community of life. I am aware of the incredible beauty, the chaos and turmoil, the lack of repetition, the continual revelation of God and the need to stop and stare, to name and proclaim. There is passion and excitement around active participation in the unfolding adventure of life and wholeness. There is also a profound sense of responsibility. By being mindful of Earth's abundant resources, which are finite, may we take to heart the need to walk lightly and in harmony. My hope is that the sharing of my experience and insights will lead those who engage with them to an extraordinary sense of the mystery of life and relationship. This in turn will lead to a profound transformation in terms of spirituality, lifestyle, work, leisure and a vibrant sense of place in the wonder of the Earth and the Universe.

# OUT OF WONDER

## Astonishment at the wonder of life

Every day I am offered the tremendous gift of sipping
from the mystery of life,
Tasting the exquisite beauty in what the universe offers
me from the vast cup of the cosmos.

Joyce Rupp

When I was a child there was something magical about stories
that began with: 'Long, long ago, there lived…' or 'Once
upon a time, when fairies roamed'. There was something
about these stories that was larger than life and, no matter
how many surprising and scary twists and turns they took, the
outcome always seemed to be hopeful. Could this be a
metaphor for the greatest story of all time, the story of the
universe? To the child's mind, long, long ago usually means
last year or at most when one's parents or teachers were
young. Now we know that it stretches all the way back to
almost fourteen billion years ago. My childhood was filled
with stories. I thought my parents knew everything. In
storytelling my father spoke with a reverence and excitement
that was infectious. During long winter nights as Inishowen
lay duveted in snow, we siblings would snuggle up in front of

our blazing hearth fire. This seemed even more cosy within earshot of the howling Atlantic waves dancing around Inishtrahull Island. The rich fullness of my father's voice filled the hushed gathering as he recounted adventures from stories he had read or created. His stories were serialised. This created an ecstasy and an agony known only to a child struggling against the overwhelming power of sleep. 'To be continued' became the 'carrot' that held us in the in-between time.

What is fact and what fiction? Are the dream world and real world such strangers to each other? Are stories timeless or are they time-bound? Is the storyteller separate from the story? To my mind stories are the energy of life, alive in themselves as well as inspiring life and meaning. Their enduring vitality is born out of a fusion of the real and the symbolic. For instance, as I sat riveted by the adventures and expeditions shared by my father, I remember being entranced by the flames sporting up and down the fire logs in our hearth. Somehow I was intuitively connecting with the larger story of life flaring forth from the original fireball all those billions of years ago. I was touching the memory of the universe. We touch this ancestral memory without being aware of it most of the time.

The memory that we, and all creatures, hold in every sinew and muscle of our beings is the story of the birth and evolution of the universe. It is our origin story. Each one of us is a particular manifestation of it. We express this wonderful unfolding story in our own unique way simply by being who we are. And strange as it may seem to us we are not alone in this great adventure. The story of the universe is being told in the miracle of sunlight, in the music of rocks, in the melody of forests, in the dance of the waters, in birdsong, in the silent labour of tiny microbes, in the exuberance of the young of all species as well as in human language, culture, song and dance. It is being woven among and between species in the wondrous web of life. This intriguing narrative is our story, the sacred story of the community of life, which is the universe.

## The Wonder of Creation

Look at a flower, an insect, fungus or water droplet under a microscope and life will never be the same. What a revelation, what magnificence! The creatures we so often dismiss as uninteresting or a nuisance, meriting only to be stamped upon, flushed down the drain or scrubbed off our walls, are so incredibly alive and beautiful when we really see them. It is only when we are fortunate enough to come face-to-face with different species that conversion takes place. The enthralling beauty of flowers, sunsets or butterflies gives us a glimpse of this. The miracle of energy, of life and kinship shines forth. Gradually we have moved away from closeness to the Earth. We need to reconnect. A leisurely stroll in the countryside along the hedgerows and byroads reveals such beauty and diversity. The wonder of life is incredibly visible, yet invisible to the naked or distracted eye. I long to live the rest of my life in growing admiration for the life forms around me. I desire to call each by name, to proclaim their wonder, whether star, plant, insect, animal or person. Perhaps a day will dawn when my eyes will be so opened in awe and gratitude that the delightful name 'eye bright' will be as true of me as it is of the wild beauty of that tiny flower. 'Come forth into the light of things, let Nature be your teacher' (William Wordsworth 1770-1850).

The sheer wonder of creation is that with our every breath we hum to the rhythm of the cosmos. To the person of faith everything speaks of God, the Great Spirit. We are made of stardust, born in swirling space and held as one in the secure lap of gravity. The bonds connecting all of life were woven in the mystery and miracle of hydrogen and shaped in the blazing heat of the original fireball. All in the total community of life were potentially present in that beginning moment, long, long ago. We have journeyed in the universe through its creative wanderings over aeons, sensing the beauty, the chaos and complexity, moments of breakthrough and breakdown, of surprise and delight as the universe continues to manifest itself in fresh ways. Annie Dillard captures this emergence in *Pilgrim at Tinker Creek*, where she speaks of 'the universe bawling with newness'.

From the beginning of time human beings have been wondering about the meaning of existence. 'Where did the universe come from?', 'Where is that place where it all began?', 'How long ago?', 'Where are we all going?', 'Is there a centre to it all?' This wonder still shines through the eyes of our children. I think of my little grandnephew, Keith. Like so many toddlers he loves water. Bath time is splash time, not to mention helping with the washing up! After Christmas dinner last year some of us decided to go for a walk on the nearby beach. The air was crisp and the wind bracing as it circled in from a north-easterly direction. Keith, with his ever increasing vocabulary exclaimed: 'W-aa-t-e-r, w-aa-t-err ... big b-aa-th', as he ran excitedly towards the incoming tide. That memory of the child's absolute delight at the sight of so much water and his way of naming it in terms of his experience illustrates how we are in terms of the new story of the universe. The sheer wonder of life is overwhelming. The image of bath and ocean portrays something of the reality of how we are in the face of mystery.

Our forebears tried to understand their surroundings with their unaided senses. They learned from their experience. They marvelled at the night sky with the Moon and stars twinkling in the darkness. Where did light come from? The Sun seemed so far distant yet its presence could be felt among the community of planet Earth. How were rocks formed and why are some clothed with soil while others lie exposed, jutting to the heavens? Did water always fall from the sky? What moved the waves and caused the winds to blow? What secrets does soil contain that enable it to produce food season after season for our nourishment? Just as in the animal species, human senses were finely tuned as people listened and observed the workings of the Earth and the greater cosmos.

They observed the changing seasons, marvelled at the interplay of light and darkness and the rhythm of birth, life, death and rebirth. Through learning to connect with the rhythms of Earth they were able to live in harmony with its processes. They came to value the need for rest in order to be revitalised through their observance of fallow time. The life-giving soil needed time to lie fallow so that its vitality might be restored for the ongoing nourishment of the community of life. The same was true for all beings including the human. The living community of the natural world shows us the art of rest and recreation. What a lesson for us today. Do we acknowledge in ourselves and in others the need for rest and recovery amid the demands of life? How faithful am I to areas of my life and work requiring time to lie fallow? Our ancestors discovered that variety is the spice of life. Where is the variety in my life and work? They learned that crop rotation was key in horticulture. What a challenge to our mono-cultural mindset! The refinement of their senses enabled our forebears to calculate distance and direction, to estimate the time and predict weather patterns with amazing accuracy.

I grew up on a farm close to a vast expanse of blanket bogland. I remember the seasons of planting and harvesting in particular. These were neighbourhood times when farming families worked together in rotation (*meitheal*). Climate and weather were crucial factors. I have this image of my father silhouetted at our back door gazing at the early night sky. After quiet reflection he would predict the weather for the following day. This was before the early Bush radio weather bulletins. Work in the fields or bog proceeded accordingly. On the farm I learned to sense the seasons, to sniff the air for rain and storms and scan the sky for snow. I developed a rudimentary knowledge of animal behaviour patterns, which warned of impending storms. Livestock could smell the rising winds and approaching rains; they moved to more sheltered areas along the hedgerows or under the trees. In the farmyard chickens scurried for cover while our family dog whined restlessly at the early signs of thunderstorms. Many people could literally feel in their bones that rain was on the way.

Why have we today moved so far from this way of being in tune with the health and vibrancy of Earth? Early farmers worked in partnership with the Earth. Seeds were saved and shared while animal manure was added to the soil to strengthen its mineral wealth. This is still the practice in some areas of our world, but alas it is being trampled out of existence in the stampede for so-called economic progress. Our forebears may not have understood the science of the universe or planet Earth, but they had an acute sense of the finiteness of existence and resources. They were aware of the need to walk lightly so that others in the community of creation might share in the miracle of life.

I remember my mother as a woman of wisdom. Home-making was her art and what an artist she was! Hospitality was her other name. I used to wonder how she managed to feed so many people, especially visitors arriving unexpectedly. Her secret lay in her respect for the Earth and its fruits, which she used in cooking, baking, jam-making and wine-processing for that special occasion. I recall her tears when Maggie, our family horse, was sold and replaced by a tractor. My mother knew the horse's worth and intuitively she sensed the beginning of a more aggressive relationship with the land. The growing human population was beginning to impact upon the land and its resources in a different way. While much of this advance in technology is for the better we know from our experience that all is not well. How we need to recover something of this sense of oneness, of intimacy and partnership with the Earth in our moment in history.

**In Touch with Mystery**
The ancient Egyptians imagined the universe as a pyramid, the earth formed the base and the heavens enclosed the four sides. Among the Hindus of old, the earth was seen as a huge plate resting on the backs of four elephants poised on a giant floating turtle.[1] The Great God Vishnu had measured out the extent of the universe in three giant strides making it the home of the gods and of humanity.[2] The earliest Indian cultures believed that Shakti, the Mother Goddess, was the source of all energy and creativity in the universe. They associated her in particular with the fertility of the earth in crop yields and food production. For the Celts of North and

Western Europe, the universe was the creative energy emanating from the Great Mother Goddess.

From earliest times people were aware from their observations that mammals (humans are one species of mammal) carried their young within their own bodies and nourished them from their own substance. From this they venerated the universe as the living body of a Goddess-Mother-Creator with all living things within her as partakers of her divinity. She was seen as the great cosmic womb birthing the atoms, stars, galaxies, oceans, plants, animals and people. This formed the basis of the earliest natural religion of humanity.[3] Gradually as the classical civilisations evolved and male images of gods emerged, there was a movement away from this kinship with the earth as the great Mother Goddess. However, it never became totally extinct, surviving especially among many indigenous peoples and communities of women. The veneration of Gaia (the Greek name for Mother Earth) is re-emerging within some monotheistic religious traditions today.

Since c. 5,000 BCE various classical religious traditions have been evolving. Each has its own way of grappling with the mystery of existence. The Christian way is summed up in the Prologue of St John's Gospel: 'In the beginning was the Word, and the Word was with God, and the Word was God. He was in the beginning with God. All things came into being through him, and without him not one thing came into being'.[4] Similar beliefs are echoed in other traditions, for example, Allah as creator in the Islamic tradition, Spider Woman as weaver of the universe among Native Americans, Brahma, creator and director of the universe in Hindu mythology and Lounnotar, the creator goddess of the Finns in Nordic mythology.

# Wonder

For almost forty thousand years people have been astonished at the miracle of life. Everywhere they experienced an awesome, wondrous sense of divine presence in the universe. This cannot be explained or adequately understood. It is mystery. What cannot be expressed through the medium of language was often proclaimed in music, dance, art and craft, home-making and silent worship. For many, an attitude of praise and prayer is the mode love takes on in the presence of mystery. One thinks of the ancient cave paintings, sun dance and earth rituals, the music of campfires celebrating the changing seasons of spring, summer, autumn and winter. The sagas and folklore of our ancestors, together with the sacred ceremonies of mosque, temple, synagogue and church brought people together in community solidarity with the reality and mystery of life, death, resurrection and reincarnation.

Today we have the benefits of scientific exploration, especially during the past four hundred years, with ever more powerful telescopes and microscopes. This practical evidence and the intuitive knowing of our forebears with their unaided senses, while shedding some light on the complexity of life, does not dispel the mystery of it all, which still continues to baffle our human consciousness. The endless wonder of life is that the more we know, the more there is to know. This challenges us towards an attitude of humility, whereby we will be forever on a voyage of discovery. Albert Einstein (1879-1955), the renowned German physicist, believed that imagination is better than knowledge. The passion of his life was to discover what the Great One thinks. Let us engage our imagination, as well as our knowledge, as we journey to the beginning of time, to the long, long ago when our universe was born.

## Notes

1. *The Ultimate Encyclopedia of Mythology* eds, Arthur Cotterell & Rachel Storm (Lorenzo Books, London, 1999) offers comprehensive information from six different regions of the world.
2. Ibid 378.
3. Hitherto unknown or ignored evidence of the goddess tradition or original natural religion of all humanity is being unearthed by archaeologists, theologians, cultural historians, poets and artists. The following are recommended: Marija Gimbutas *The Language of the Goddess* (HarperCollins, 1991); Mary Condren *The Serpent and the Goddess* (Harper & Row, San Francisco, 1989); Monica Sjoo & Barbara Mor *The Great Cosmic Mother* (Harper & Row, San Francisco, 1987) and Matthew Fox *One River, Many Wells* (Gateway, Ireland, 2001).
4. John 1:1-3 *The Bible: New Revised Standard Version* (American Bible Society, New York, 1989).

# Out of Emptiness – Life in a Fireball

## Birthing of Stars and Galaxies

Child there is a light somewhere
Under a star,
Sometime it will be for you
A window that looks
Inward to God.
                    Patrick Kavanagh

Stars hold a special fascination for children. Perhaps they sense our common origin. From time to time the child within each of us awakens to the glow of this kinship. When I was a child I marvelled at the abundance of sky like a huge dome covering the earth. Somehow it seemed close, with neither the Sun nor the Moon and stars strangers in far distant places. In the wild freedom of my childhood I used to converse with them. I sensed I was not alone whether sitting on our doorstep or lying on my back in the big meadow beside the house squinting at the Sun. It was so exciting when the Sun would wink through the passing clouds. Likewise with the Moon and stars. I still remember the warmth of snuggling up in bed gazing at the Moon and stars beckoning through our tiny bedroom window.

Did the Sun rest while I slept? Was the Moon the mother star surrounded by her multitude of starry children? There was a special glow between us on frosty nights, as the stars seemed to edge even closer. Even on the darkest nights when the stars were hiding I used to sense their presence and darkness didn't seem too dark anymore. There was an affinity there that even the blackest night could not dispel. It was something I took for granted. Now I am awakening to the scientific fact of our common origin, the truth that we belong together in the community we call life.

## Imagine the Miracle Moment

What do we mean by our common origin? For centuries, women and men have pondered the birthing of stars. What are they made of? How are we related? Is it true that every being in all of creation is made of stardust? When we consider the web of life and all the creatures of all species it becomes more obvious that all beings are interconnected and dependent one on the other – bacteria, plants, insects, animals, birds and people. However, we humans tend to think of ourselves as self-sufficient, especially with our ever-emerging technologies. Some believe the human to be a separate creation from all other beings, seeing us *apart from* rather than *a part of* the total community of life. This is potentially harmful to us and to the balance of life's resources, which are being progressively undermined by our attitudes and behaviour. I believe we need to rediscover our sense of place 'in the family of things' (*Wild Geese* by Mary Oliver). Ours is the first generation to have the combined wisdom of our ancestors – still alive among indigenous peoples, especially – and the discoveries of science, to enable us to re-member our true identity as cosmic beings.

# Emptiness

The story of the universe being told today offers a new transforming context for our lives, our hopes and our dreams. The understanding of this story is crucial in enabling us to move beyond human concerns alone and to embrace the entire community of the universe. Why is it important, indeed urgent, that we do this? The evolutionary story of life affirms that we are one, a unity. We belong together. It is not possible to live in isolation from other beings. The oneness of all life is our context. The Buddhists speak of 'co-dependent arising': 'When the sun rises, green shoots appear, leaves unfurl, flowers bud and fruit is formed. With the sun, birds rise; with the sun, people rise; all rise together. Everyone's rising depends on everyone else's rising'.[1]

The magnificent story of life and our place within it is known as 'cosmology'. The birth moment is often referred to as the 'Big Bang' because of the explosion of a highly condensed mass in millions of degrees of heat. Some physicists prefer to call this the flaring forth of the original fireball. We are told that in the beginning, long, long ago, there was literally nothing, not even space. Emptiness or nothingness is difficult to imagine: 'nature abhors a vacuum'. The emergence of life as we know it from the 'empty void' is mysterious. From a religious perspective it is the stuff of faith, the acknowledgement of a Supreme Being, who creates out of nothingness. Today with the aid of scientific evidence and quantum mechanics we are being challenged to look more creatively at what is meant by empty space or vacuum.[2] Is it really *empty*? Brian Swimme, in his book *The Hidden Heart of the Cosmos*, describes this emptiness thus: 'The ground of the universe is an empty fullness, a fecund nothingness'.[3] Within Hindu and Buddhist thinking there is a term, *sunya*, which refers to a full void. The void is 'empty' because it has no things in it in the tangible sense, but is nonetheless full because it is the fertile womb from which all things emerge and to which all returns. *Sunya* is both nothingness and fullness, the empty void holding the potential for everything that will ever come to exist.

## A Long Memory

From this emptiness there came into being a tiny speck of fiery space that contained sufficient energy to create all the trillions of galaxies and stars that twinkle in the sky. And that is not all, for contained in that primordial speck was all the energy to direct the expansion of the universe ever since. And if that is not mystery enough, what about the fact that we, each one of us, were also potentially present at that moment of flaring forth of the original fireball? The birthing of existence and time are simultaneous. Particles of light as well as time emerged in the beginning. All that has been, is, and will be was contained in the miracle of hydrogen.

For the briefest moment all was hydrogen, which, in the presence of millions of degrees of heat, fused into helium releasing massive amounts of energy that caused the stars to shine. The nuclear transformations occurring in stars led to the formation of other elements, for example, carbon, nitrogen, oxygen and so on. Elements are composed of atoms and some combine to form compounds, for example, hydrogen and oxygen in the formation of water. This first element, hydrogen, held within itself everything else that would be the universe, which is still evolving. Perhaps we can better understand this if we think of the power of seeds. The banyan tree is enormous, made up of more than a thousand trunks. I recall standing beside one of these majestic trees in northern Jamaica and wondering how on earth such massiveness could have evolved from a tiny seed. Indeed I never felt so close to my kin in the microbial community! If I hold an acorn in my hand, do I pause to acknowledge that a huge oak tree is coded within it? When I handle the tiniest of seeds I'm in touch with mystery.

## Atoms to Anatomies

Everything in creation is, as it were, a community of atoms: the soil beneath us, the sky life above us, the communities that are oceans, the tools we use, our own bodies. Atoms, which are the building blocks of life, are so small that they are unrecognisable except with the aid of extremely high-powered microscopes. One could fit up to a billion atoms on a full stop at the end of a sentence. Yet atoms consist largely of empty space, space dotted with tinier clouds of energy known as sub-atomic particles. Hydrogen, the simplest in terms of atomic structure, is the lightest and most abundant gas in the universe.

Until recently, scientists worked on the theory that atoms were matter, an atom was understood to be purely physical, a small inert piece of matter, in fact the tiniest subdivision, which has all the properties of the element.[4] It lasts forever and could not be sub-divided. The ancient Greek world, from which we in the Western world draw our cosmology or origin story, differentiated between spirit and matter. Humans alone among species were believed to have the inner dimension – spirit. Ernest Rutherford, New Zealand-British physicist, managed to split the nucleus of the atom in 1919. What a revelation was to follow: the atom was not made of inert matter, rather inside was a universe so vast and deep that it can only be compared to the outer universe. Physicists are scarcely able to articulate this phenomenon. The implications are unfolding, they are profound, even mystical.

## A Very Long Way to Stardom

On special family occasions many people like to reminisce about times past and recall what is often scant knowledge of the life and legacy of their ancestors. As we embark on this journey to the beginning of the universe and existence, I invite you, the reader, to expand the notion of ancestry, to transcend human boundaries in our search for identity and meaning. Our human story is integral to the universe story. Our ancestral heritage is literally within the flaring forth almost 14 billion years ago. We emanate from stars, formed from the Earth, which was birthed from exploding stars in the creation of the Solar System. I am made of stardust, a child of the universe. Let us reconnect with our true lineage and celebrate, overawed in the knowledge that it took billions of years of creative genius before the human emerged some time between 2.6 and 7 million years ago.

## Universal Hospitality

The integrity of the sacred universe story embraces all our stories, honours them and situates them in context, the expanded context of the entire community of all creation. Whether I'm an Irish Christian, an Afghan Muslim, an Australian Aborigine, the wind that rustles the autumn leaves, an Indian Hindu, an asylum-seeker, a salmon riding the waves, a member of the Travelling Community, an African-American citizen, the cuckoo that heralds summer, the tiny microbes that labour in the dark soil beneath our feet, all of us sing from the same hymn sheet, the glorious anthem, the song that is the universe. Every member of every species has a unique note in the symphony. Sometimes we can be tempted to change the script, to adapt to our logic and reasoning, to construe it in order to score a philosophical or theological point. It is vital that we respect and value the integrity of the universe story, the creation of divine genius. Nothing less than our own integrity and that of all life in its manifold expression is at stake:

> Presently we are returning to the primordial community of the universe, the earth, and all living beings. Each has its own voice, its role, its power over the whole. But, most important, each has its special symbolism. The excitement of life is in the numinous experience wherein we are given to each other in that larger celebration of existence in which all things attain their highest expression, for the universe, by definition, is a single gorgeous celebratory event.[5]

Our life, our very existence, and that of all beings, is rooted in the generativity that gave birth to the universe in the beginning. Let us look then at our cosmological lineage, the energy, the creativity, chaos and unfolding complexities out of which we emerged:

> The Cosmos is all that is or ever was or ever will be. The feeblest contemplations of the Cosmos stir in us – there is a tingling in the spine, a catch in the voice, a faint sensation, as if a distant memory, of falling from a height. We know we are approaching the greatest of mysteries.[6]

On a timescale of 13 billion years, planet Earth was formed around 4.5 billion years ago while humans emerged over 2.6 million years ago. Taking the image of a day, we arrived close to midnight! The human is that being in whom the universe becomes conscious of and celebrates itself in conscious self-awareness. I am the universe, in all its beauty and creativity, become aware of itself in its 13 billion years of unbroken evolutionary journey. What an awesome thought. The indigenous peoples of South America believe that in order to become human one must make room in oneself for the immensities of the universe. The astronomer looking through a telescope is the universe looking at itself, or my little grandnephew entranced by the immensity of the ocean is the earth enraptured by itself. Similarly, when one praises the Great Spirit, the Creator, one becomes the voice of the universe celebrating the mystery of itself and the wonder of existence. I have often wondered at the mystery of creation, which is not a once off event in the distant past by a distant deity, but a continuous process in which all creatures are involved:

> The Word is living, being, spirit, all verdant greening, all creativity. This word manifests itself in every creature.[7]

### The Gravity of it All

Beginning as pure energy emerging from the quantum vacuum, 'the all nourishing abyss,'[8] the universe evolved from the early atoms of hydrogen and helium, to stars and galaxies, molecules, cells, plants, fish, insects, birds, animals and people. Everything in the universe is held in unity by four invisible forces, four tendencies or behaviours of atoms.

These are: gravity, electromagnetism and the strong and weak nuclear forces.[9] Gravity is about mutual attraction, the mutual attraction between every single piece of matter in the entire universe. The greater the mass and energy the stronger is the attraction. The Sun is so massive that its pull can be felt over millions of kilometres of space. The Earth is smaller and orbits round the Sun, while the Moon is smaller again, its gravity weaker, and orbits round the Earth.

The creative tension of these four invisible tendencies holding the universe in a simple, unbroken process from the beginning enables atoms to enter into relationships that have the capacity to create new compounds without annihilating each other in the process. When hydrogen and oxygen, for example, enter into relationship, the chaos that ensues produces change, which in this instance emerges as water. Hydrogen remains hydrogen, and oxygen is still oxygen, both are intact, yet together they have created water. The coming together into relationship has activated, has triggered, the creative potential each has, but unaware of before interacting. And so the process continues with atomic fruitfulness underlining the fact that the universe is one, is a communion of diverse subjects. The graced activity of these four tendencies operating in harmony enables the universe to remain united with itself as it diversifies – to be one, an interacting unity with itself, a uni-verse. What a lesson for us humans with our latent creative energy, both among ourselves and in the wider communion of all life.

Are these merely hard scientific facts or have they anything to communicate to us humans? In light of the fact that the universe is evolving in a sequence of irreversible transformations from the beginning, can there be room for a radical discontinuity between the natural and human world? We are different beings, but not separate in the web of life. In his examination of the basic laws in the fundamental ordering of the universe, cultural historian and geologian, Thomas Berry, explains the presence of three guiding principles or tendencies, namely, differentiation, interiority and communion. He sees the universe as one single community of life, a sacred community. This is his core belief. The primary bonding in the physical order is through gravitational attraction and this primordial relationship finds its fulfilment in the relationships that living beings have for each other, and finally in the order of human affection.[10]

These relationships of mutuality are at the heart of the universe. Is there a challenge here for us in terms of the ideal of harmony in right relations: with ourselves, God or Supreme Being, other people and all of creation? In light of this intrinsic bonding can there be hierarchies of gender, class, ethnicity, sexual orientation, creed or species? What might form the rationale for perpetuating such inequalities? It is quite overwhelming to ponder the truth that the greater the mass and energy, the stronger the attraction. And sobering to ask: Is my/our love and care such that its influence attracts our kin in the whole community of life and sets all in orbit around the magnetic embrace of our Creator? The profound words of Teilhard de Chardin are timely:

> What we are more or less lacking at this moment is a new definition of holiness.[11]

## Passion for Creativity

In the initial seconds of birthing the universe was a million times hotter than the centre of our Sun today. For some 300,000 years, matter and radiation co-mingled. As expansion continued the temperature began to drop to that currently found on the surface of the Sun. This was a period of transformation, from nuclear particles to the first atoms of hydrogen and helium. This dynamic of transformation continued, first forming stars, galaxies and supernovae, then molecules and cells, and so into the myriad life forms populating the cosmos today: the human, the Atlantic Ocean, the song thrush, the badger and the gorse extravagance yellowing the countryside, all relishing the gift of the Sun some 250,000 kilometres away. This is indeed revelatory, all creativity, all life, reaching from the depths of ultimate mystery.

The universe continues to expand in all directions. How do we know this? In 1929, US astronomer, Edwin Hubble (from whom the Hubble Telescope takes its name), provided empirical evidence that the universe is expanding. Through his powerful telescope in California, Hubble, who had several years earlier discovered that there are many galaxies apart from our own Milky Way, further shows that these other galaxies are moving away from us, therefore the universe must be getting bigger. What Hubble was seeing had in fact been predicted by Einstein some years before. However, so overwhelmed was he by what his equations were registering, that he doctored them – a fact that he later acknowledged with regret.

Scientists tell us that the rate of expansion of the universe from the beginning moment was delicately balanced. This enabled life to emerge in its beauty and complexity. The abundance of life forms dancing in the universe are a result of the rate of expansion and the power of gravitation working in harmony from the beginning. They explain that if the rate of expansion was to decrease by even a trillionth of a trillionth of a per cent, the universe would very soon collapse, probably after a million years of expansion. In this expanding universe if the movement of the super-clusters were to be reversed they would all revert back to a single place at the same time, the so-called 'Big Crunch'. Brian Swimme uses the image of raisin bread to convey the fact that the universe is omni-centric, every place in the universe is the centre of the universe. Every raisin in the dough represents a super-cluster of galaxies. When you bake it the cake rises. If you are on any one raisin looking around, all the other raisins are moving away from you.[12] Sometimes we may think of ourselves as outside looking on. There is no such space as outside the universe: space, time, energy, creativity, chaos, all life, all of us beings are together in the universe. This is ancient wisdom, deep within our ancestral psyche: 'my body is the universe, the universe is my body'. The challenge is to enter into the universe, to become integral to and not apart from our deepest roots, the holy ground upon which we live.

Between 10 and 14 billion years ago the universe burst forth as giant galactic clouds of hydrogen and helium, this was a new force in the emerging universe:

> The dynamic of a power evoking beings with new modes of power happened both in the birth of the primordial atoms and in the birth of the galaxies and is a fundamental theme throughout fifteen billion years of cosmic development.[13]

The first galaxies and stars were formed from curdled lumps of clouds of hydrogen and helium. From these stars are born. Clumps of gas are drawn together by the force of their own gravity, the centre is pressured so much that temperatures reach about 10 million degrees centigrade, thereby initiating a nuclear fusion reaction, the clump condenses and becomes a glowing star. This is a further development of the original fireball, in turn each of us is a further expression of the fireball, we are potentially present through all the stages of evolving creativity. This is our cosmic lineage. I have this image of a troupe of dancers in diaphanous gowns waving long scarves of finest silk as they move to the rhythm of the universe. Feelings of awe and gratitude well up within me as a still, small voice proclaims my name. I am no longer an onlooker, but a participant:

> Whoever you are, no matter how lonely, the world offers itself to your imagination, calls to you like wild geese, harsh and exciting – over and over announcing your place in the family of things.[14]

The original flaring forth, the primordial blaze, extinguished itself after the fireball ended with the creation of hydrogen atoms. When one gazes at the night sky and beholds some of the billions of twinkling specks of light one could be forgiven for thinking of stars as tiny. They are in fact huge, fiery balls of gas shining millions and millions of kilometres away. How numerous are the stars? It is difficult to say with any great accuracy because most are so far distant from the naked eye. Astronomers estimate that there are about 200 billion- billion. The surface temperature of stars ranges from 3,500 °C to over 40,000 °C.

37

### Holding On – In the Milky Way

A galaxy is a massive collection of billions of stars. Galaxies are clustered together in groups of anything from less than a dozen to several thousand scattered unevenly through the universe. Our galaxy is called The Milky Way (the word 'galaxy' comes from the Greek word for milky); it almost looks as if someone spilled milk across the sky. It comprises some 100 billion stars and has a diameter of a million trillion kilometres. Prior to the 1930s, it was generally thought that there was only one galaxy, The Milky Way, but with ever more sophisticated equipment, astronomers and scientists are frequently revising ideas and beliefs. We now know that our galaxy is but one of billions adorning the universe. Each galaxy contains billions of stars. Our galaxy belongs to a neighbourhood cluster of some 3,000 galaxies, known as the Local Group, the Andromeda galaxy is the largest in this group. The Milky Way is a spiral galaxy and the Earth is a little over half way out along one of its spiral arms, about 30,000 light years from the centre.[15] This gives some faint idea of the magnitude of our galaxy, which is merely one of billions lighting up the sky.

### Blacker Than Black – The Core of Galaxies

The core of galaxies examined to date by astronomers is dominated by super-massive Black Holes. These are places where the pull of gravity is so strong that it sucks in everything, including light, hence the blackness. No one has ever seen a Black Hole, but it is thought that a star or galaxy becomes so dense that it collapses under the pull of its own gravity and shrinks to a single tiny point of infinite density known as a singularity. Stephen Hawking was influential in convincing astronomers that Black Holes, which had been already suggested, could really exist. In July 2004 Hawking admitted that he made a mistake regarding black holes. Black holes mangle or change information that falls into them rather than obliterate it as his earlier theory suggested. During the past seventy years, beginning with Jansky in 1932, the quest for the core of The Milky Way Galaxy has continued. It is now known that a massive black hole lurks right at the centre of our galaxy, containing a mass 2.6 million times that of the Sun, but taking up proportionately little space. However, the nature of this phenomenon remains a mystery, the violent and dark heart of the galaxy continues to tantalise astronomers.[16] 'What a time to be alive! Humankind has dawning upon its consciousness a new perception of its origins – the nature of life, the world, the Universe, God' (Douglas Bowman). In the next section we will turn to the Sun to shed its radiant light on the mystery of life.

## Notes

1. Satish Kumar *You Are Therefore I Am*, 177, (Green Books Ltd. Totnes, Devon, UK, 2002).
2. Quantum mechanics describes phenomena in their tiniest scales, smaller than can be seen with the naked eye. As such it modified classical mechanics (Newton). Quantum mechanics underlies the whole of modern chemistry and material science as well as being a major influence in astronomy. With a deeper understanding of how atoms, the basic building blocks of matter, behave, we are better able to understand how they bond together to form the variety/diversity of materials surrounding us.
3. Brian Swimme *The Hidden Heart of the Cosmos*, 93, (Orbis Books, Maryknoll, New York, 1996).
4. Matter has three states, namely, solid, liquid and gas. Most of the matter or substance in the universe is inside stars like the Sun.

5. Thomas Berry *The Dream of the Earth*, 5, (Sierra Club Books, San Francisco, 1988).
6. Carl Sagan *Cosmos*, 20, (Macdonald & Co. Publishers, Great Britain, 1981).
7. Hildegarde of Bingen.
8. Brian Swimme *The Hidden Heart of the Cosmos*, 100, (Orbis Books, Maryknoll, New York, 1996).
9. See Stephen Hawking *A Brief History of Time*, Ch.5 for a description of these forces. (Space Time Publications, 1988).
10. Thomas Berry 'The Primordial Imperative' in *Earth Ethics* (Vol.3 No. 2 Winter 1992, Center for Respect of Life and Environment, Washington, DC).
11. *Human Energy*, Teilhard de Chardin (Harcourt Brace Jovanovich, 1969) as quoted in *Original Blessings* by *Matthew Fox*, 108.
12. Brian Swimme *Canticle to the Cosmos* Tape One 'The Story of Our Time' 1990. *New Story Project*, Tides Foundation, San Francisco, CA 94109.
13. Brian Swimme & Thomas Berry, *The Universe Story*, 34, (HarperSanFrancisco, 1994).
14. Mary Oliver 'Wild Geese' in *New and Selected Poems*, 110, (Beacon Press, Boston, 1992).
15. It is known that light can travel at about 300,000 km per second, therefore a manageable way of measuring the speed of light is to talk of light years i.e. the distance travelled by light in one year.
16. 'Learning to Weigh the Gravitational Monsters in the Universe' in *Science Today*, *The Irish Times* June 19, 2000, Dublin, Ireland.

# OUT OF FIRE

## Birthing of the Sun and Solar System

And every child of ours needs to learn the simple truth:
She is the energy of the Sun.
And we adults should organise things so her face shines
with the same radiant joy.
                              Brian Swimme

'For the rest of my life, I want to reflect on what light is' (Albert
Einstein). We generally take light for granted as we go about our
daily lives, but we would not be alive without it. Since the
beginning of time people have been intrigued by light. The
ancient Greeks regarded light as a sort of feeler going out from
the eye, which touched objects. Hundreds of years later this
view was corrected when it was established that light was
reflected from objects onto the eye. Light is a type of energy
created by a combination of electrical and magnetic fields. It is
difficult to understand. Scientists have come to accept that light
moves both as particles and as waves. Nothing moves faster
than light. Life is filled with its presence and elusiveness. I love
walking in the woods. I recall being captivated as a child by the
streams of light shining through the thick canopies. There was
magic in the glow of sunshine splashing through the otherwise

cool shade created by the close-knit forest community. I even aspired to catching the light, but alas it proved as elusive as catching hold of air or grasping that crock of gold at the end of the rainbow!

There is a vivid sense of vitality, of music and relaxation in the forest, a feasting of one's senses. It is a place in which to pause and salute multitudes of mute friends – microbes, plants, insects, trees and birds – to return the gaze of millions of eyes. Our forest friends are deemed mute only because we are generally deaf to their voices. I sometimes try to imagine what might be stirring in and among this local community of life about me as I enter, especially when I persist in communicating with myself. There are times when I like to close my eyes in order to activate my lazier senses relishing the crumpled feeling of bark, the velvety leaves, the woody odours and mossy fragrances. The forest pathway is soft and earthy while the bony roots create a sense of timelessness. The vibrancy of life in the forest community can restore a sense of perspective especially when one is feeling overwhelmed or exhausted by the ups and downs of life. The silence, animated with birdsong, is so refreshing and one becomes aware of being rooted deep in the earth and at the same time there is the sense of reaching beyond oneself to the light, warmth and communion of earth and sky. The interplay of light and shade has echoes deep within the human psyche. There is a connection here inviting us to enter ever more rhythmically into the dance of life.

Light has emerged as a supreme symbol of life and meaning among the major philosophical and religious traditions of the world. Inspired by the miracle of sunlight and moonlight many have sought enlightenment about the mysteries of life through meditation, poetry, art, scientific research and so on. With the more recent realisation that we are made of stardust, might this be the dawning of a more sparkling attitude to life? Stars twinkle in our eyes, our smile, our thoughts, feelings, hopes and dreams. God is often referred to as *Light* and in the Christian tradition Jesus proclaims himself as 'the light of the world' (John 9:5), the one who dispels all darkness. People are exhorted to 'let your light shine', 'walk in the light' and the ultimate prayer is 'let perpetual light shine upon them' as we remember our deceased members.

### The First Ray of Sunshine

What is the source of light and why is it important? The original fireball billowing from the tiniest pinprick of energy contained all the light and potential for everything that would ever come to be. How mysterious: everything that has been, is, or ever will be was contained within the miracle of hydrogen over 13 billion years ago. Have you ever wondered why the night sky is ablaze with stars while by day we see but one, the Sun? Does this mean that the Sun is special, larger than other stars? Astronomers describe the Sun as an average star in mid-life stage, one of at least a hundred billion stars that make up our Milky Way Galaxy. Our galaxy is only one of billions of other galaxies, which make up the universe. This is difficult to imagine. It reminds me of walking on the beach and picking up a handful of sand. As I isolate and allow the tiny grains of rock to sift through my fingers I can only shake my head in disbelief in light of the fact that all the grains of sand that ever were or are cannot equal this great spectacle. And these galaxies combined form but a tiny fraction of deep space. I find this fascinating, indeed overwhelming. The Sun is our nearest star, a mere 150 million kilometres (93 million miles) from the Earth compared to the next nearest star, Proxima Centauri, which is 250,000 times further from the Earth than the Sun. The fact of the Sun's relative closeness makes for its magnificence and prominence in our sky and establishes it as a stable source of energy to sustain life on earth by powering the behaviour of the earth's atmosphere, creating rain, wind and ocean currents.

The Milky Way, formed over 10 billion years ago, is the birthplace of the Sun. Stars are essentially huge balls of hot gas fuelled by nuclear reactions deep within their cores. These reactions fuse hydrogen and helium during the main lifetime of the star. Gradually as the star grows old, this initial phase gives way to the development of a giant, which converts helium into carbon and various other heavier elements. At the end of their main sequence lifetimes, stars swell to become giants and super-giants. Massive stars die in what is known as a 'supernova explosion', a spectacular billowing of hot gas and dust, which finishes off a super-giant star.

Scientists believe that our Sun was birthed in such an explosion about 4.6 billion years ago. As the infant Sun started to become a fully-fledged star, the remaining material from its birth moment was left orbiting the Sun at frenzied speed creating a solar nebula – a cooling disc-like form of gas and dust. Gradually specks of dust began to fuse together to form tiny rocks, which in time joined together to form larger bodies surrounded by clouds of gas. Those formed in the warm inner areas of the disc became the small rocky planets: Mercury, Venus, Earth and Mars. Jupiter and Saturn, the fifth and sixth planets out from the Sun, are the giants of the Solar System. Uranus, Neptune and Pluto are the outer planets; these were completely unknown in ancient times.[1] Since the 1960s, with the acceleration of space travel, numerous space-probes have been dispatched to study the Sun and Solar System. These have revealed extraordinary details of complex atmospheres and hierarchies of worlds: satellites, asteroids and comets. Satellites are celestial bodies orbiting a planet, separate from it, but held by gravity, for example, the Moon and planet earth. Within the Solar System, besides the Sun, planets and their moons, are numerous lumps of rock and ice. The largest of these rocky boulders are known as asteroids or meteorites. Ceres, the largest known, measures up to one thousand kilometres in diameter. Most are located in a broad ring about midway between the orbits of Mars and Jupiter. Comets are lumps of dust and ice found in the outermost parts of our Solar System. Halley's Comet is probably the most famous of all the comets; it was visible to the naked eye in 1986. Perhaps even more familiar is Hale-Bopp, seen more brightly in 1997.

## Moonlight on Planet Earth
'What is there in thee, moon, that thou shouldst move my heart so potently?' (John Keats: *Endymion, III*). The Moon is the Earth's natural satellite. It is thought that the Moon was formed as a result of a high-impact collision between Earth and another planet during the initial stages of the evolution of the Solar System. The Moon is a ball of rock about one-quarter the size of Earth held in its orbit by mutual gravitational attraction. This force also means that the Moon follows the Earth as it orbits the Sun. Between 1969 and 1972 some twelve astronauts have walked on the moon and experienced the lunar landscape of massive mountain ranges, huge craters and wide valleys.

Isaac Newton (1642–1727) developed the law of gravitation and laws of motion. He found that forces always occur in pairs – action and reaction. His Third Law of Motion states that: 'For every action (force) there is an equal and opposite reaction (force)'.[2] Applying this to the Earth-Moon relationship, one sees that since the Earth exerts gravitational force on the Moon to keep it in orbit therefore the Moon must exert an opposite pull on the Earth. This is what causes tides in our oceans. The Moon's gravity gathers the oceans into an oval shape around the Earth, creating a bulge of water on each side of the world. As the Earth spins round on its axis each day, different parts of its surface are closer to the Moon. The water in the oceans on the side of the Earth nearest the Moon is attracted to the Moon more powerfully than that further away thus causing high tide as opposed to low tide.

When I gaze into the night sky the Moon is by far the brightest of the heavenly bodies. Interestingly, the Moon has no light of its own. Moonlight is simply the Sun's light reflected off the white dusty surface of the Moon. The Moon is visible to us only because it reflects light. During each month, the Moon undergoes various changes, known as phases, these follow the sequence from 'new' moon to 'full' moon as different amounts of the Moon's sunlit face becomes visible to us as it orbits the Earth. And so it is with us human beings, we too reflect the Sun's light, the divine illumination flooding all spheres of existence. Anne Primavesi, in her book, *Gaia's Gift*,[3] calls us to our senses so that before it is too late 'we may perceive that it is only in the light illuminating earth as a whole that we may truly see ourselves'.

# Fire

## Humans Light Up for the First Time

Humans discovered fire some 500,000 years ago during the early Palaeolithic period.[4] The art of fire-making is one distinction between humans and animals. Those primitive sparks fanned into flame have ignited civilisations ever since with generation after generation gathering around the fire, whether inside or outdoors, for shelter, sustenance, song, dance and celebration. The first night fires were the moon and stars dazzling the heavens. Our ancestors were fascinated by these heavenly bodies, hence the howling of the wolf at the moonlit sky, the astrological signs of the Zodiac, like the Water-carrier, Crab, Pisces and Virgo, Greek heroes like Perseus and Orion, and the Dragon constellation of the Babylonians.

Fire is at the heart of the earth, as we know from volcanic eruptions when raging hot molten lava spews out from fire-mountains across the globe. Many ancient peoples believed that gods lived inside these fire mountains. Consequently, they kept drawing close to the mountain edge to soil made fertile by the lava eruptions, god's beneficence, despite the danger of more fiery outbursts. In Co. Louth, Sliabh Foye, the Fire Mountain, rising up in the Carlingford Peninsula, is like a beacon or watchful eye across land and sea. Its craggy summit represents the eroded roots of what was an active volcano about sixty million years ago.

Fire is a potent symbol in religious ritual and rites of passage with emphasis on its purifying and transforming powers, for example, the Paschal Fire in the Christian Easter ceremonies and funeral pyre ceremony in the Hindu tradition. It has been to the fore in times of persecution and death – the burning at the stake of Joan of Arc, and of the countless women during the notorious 'witch hunts' which spread across Europe just a few hundred years ago. These were in response to false allegations against women healers and counsellors. Throughout history heroic endeavours are described as being inspired by the fire of passion. That fire burning within has the potential to inspire good or ill in its all-consuming ferocity: violence, manipulation and control, or the pursuit of freedom, justice and well-being among the entire community of creation.

## The Hearth – Centre of Gravity

In Ireland as elsewhere the hearth fire has for centuries been the centre of light, energy, warmth and nurturance. *'Níl aon tinteán mar do thinteán féin'*, 'there is no fireside like your own fireside'. In hundreds of locations throughout the country there are the archaeological remains of what are known as *'fulacht fiadh'* or deer roast. These Bronze Age (c. 2000–500 BCE) cooking sites were an integral part of everyday life and are sometimes discovered near Stone Circles, like at Drombeag in Glandore in West Cork. They consist of a trough and hearth. Hot stones from the hearth are placed in the trough to boil water for household needs. Scores more of these sites are being unearthed as bulldozers ravish our landscape in the aftermath of the so-called Celtic Tiger.

In more recent centuries, before electricity or gas became commonplace, the hearth fire provided the heat, and even lighting, as well as the energy to bake our bread and cook our food. In the home, particularly in rural Ireland, the hearth was the centre of gravity, the robust symbol of hospitality. Here was shelter and ease from the cold winds and rainy days, the place of togetherness for family, friends and strangers. It was the seat of storytelling, of neighbourhood gossip and musings about life, about destiny, about faith and provided a cosy backdrop for the eventide family rosary with its particular litany of prayer intentions. Candlelight, as an extension of the hearth, lit up the dark and eerie spaces with its flickering flame, casting shadows as imagination thrived in the whispering blackness. The hearth fire was larger than human concerns, it often sheltered and nurtured the farm animals and provided some of their food especially in lean winter months. The hearth space was often home to cat, dog and baby lamb or pig, as well as humans.

### Ériu – Ancient Irish Goddess of the Hearth

The hearth belongs to an ancient tradition in the Irish context. Long before the Celts came (between 500 and 300 BCE) Ireland was divided geographically into four provinces around a central life-giving, mythical point intrinsic to the sacred whole. This was basic in Irish mythology. The fifth province was named 'Mide', meaning 'neck' or 'middle', connecting the body of Ériu throughout the island of Ireland. This was holy ground on which people could encounter the goddesses and gods. Ireland was named after a living goddess, Ériu of the Tuatha De Danaan. Ériu, the daughter of Cesair and granddaughter of Bith,[5] is a triple goddess, her 'sisters' being Banba and Fódla. Together they were synonymous with Ireland in its entirety:

> In her name every province had a place. She was their collective origin and product, the comprehensive landlady, who built, owned, named, and lived in the island home.[6]

Fintan, uncle of Ériu, is identified with Sliabh Uisnig, Ireland's central mountain and specifically with a limestone glacial boulder on Uisneach hill, Aill na Mireann (the Stone of

Divisions). Uisneach lies a few miles from the town of
Mullingar, Co. Westmeath. He planted a tree there – Craeb
Uisnig – and around it planted four berries at distances of
twenty miles. In this way he set up four territorial divisions
with Uisneach as a mythical fifth, known as *'umbilicus
Hiberniae'*, 'the umbilical cord of Ireland'. Mide, Eriu's foster-
son, took over Uisneach from Fintan so that Uisneach, Aill na
Mireann and Mide became synonymous with the mythical
fifth province to which he gave his name. Ériu gave us the gift
of fire through her foster-son Mide, the first man to light a
fire in Ireland. He kindled this fire near Uisneach from his
foster-mother's central hearth and it blazed for seven years.
From the hearth of Ériu every fire in Ireland was lit. The
hearth fire at Uisneach could be seen on mountains and
hilltops in some twenty counties:

> Ériu's bonfire map linked province to nation, home to
> island, and individual to godhead.[7]

### The Sun is in the Eye
In old Irish, the word *'súil'* means 'eye' and 'sun'. In pondering
this connection I am reminded of Brian Swimme's
explanation of light and how beings capture photons of
light from the Sun. The fact that light is visible to us
humans is because of the miracle of photosynthesis when
plants, aided by the chlorophyll molecule, learned to
capture the Sun some 3.9 billion years ago. He explains that
the retinal molecule in the eye is one half of beta-carotene,
which is a molecule like chlorophyll, so when we open our
eyes we can see with the same process used by plants to
capture the Sun:

If the earth hadn't worked this out, nothing would have taken place. The earth conformed to the nature of the sun. So the sun is captured in the chlorophyll molecule. Likewise with the retinal molecule. *The sun is in the eye.*[8]

This is consonant with the mythic tradition. The divine intelligence, *súil*, integrates with the eyes of all beings: fish, insect, bird, animal and person, thereby entering the whole being – head and heart – and dispelling any separations. What a powerful affirmation of the communion of all life. In that tradition Ériu's hearth blazing as the fire of Uisneach was the eye of Ireland, where Ériu was perceived to be at home across the hills and fields of the entire country:

> Eye symbols, engraved in the fourth millennium BC as part of the original iconography of several Irish monuments, show the presence of the 'eye goddess' in Ireland.[9]

Brigid was an ancient Irish Triple Goddess whose three persons were identified with poetry, healing and smithcraft. She was the goddess of wisdom, fertility and home-making. She was especially a fire goddess, guardian of the hearth, and associated with ritual fires of purification, healing and inspiration. There was the fire of Brigid burning through the centuries until it was stamped out during allegations of paganism in the thirteenth century and later during the spread of the Protestant Reformation in the sixteenth century. In recent years it has been rekindled by some of Brigid's followers, the Brigidine Sisters. During the annual Brigid celebrations, which coincide with the beginning of the Celtic season of Imbolc,[10] this fire burns brightly in Kildare Town Square. Brigid's fire belongs to a more ancient tradition, the Roman Goddess Vesta, who, with her followers the Vestal Virgins, tended the sacred flame of the hearth.

There were the druidic fires epitomised on the Hill of Tara, Co. Meath, one of the seats of the High Kings.[11] In the fourth century, St Patrick and his followers lit an Easter fire on the nearby Hill of Slane. This was in opposition to the druidic fire and marked the beginning of Christianity in Ireland. Local people continue this Easter tradition of gathering on the Hill of Slane.

## Hearth Moments
The hearth, as well as being a place of warmth and light, was also a centre of communing, of silence, of contemplation. The music of the flames circle dancing and the quiet peace of red-hot embers turning ashen made for soul, for inspiration and contentment. Who among us cannot recall special hearth moments? Perhaps the smell of burning turf or logs, cricket song, quiet moments alone, laughter and conversation before bedtime or the music of celebrations. For some there may even be the memory of tobacco or snuff mingling with the welcoming odour of burning peat. Even with our advanced technologies, which thankfully afford more comfort and less labour, many people continue to create a hearth space in their home, a place to slow down, to relax and commune in an increasingly economy driven world, so hyped with frenetic activity and juggling of values.

## The Sun – Hearth of the Universe
I believe that the hearth fire symbolises a much greater fire in our lives as the entire community of life, namely, the Sun.

# Fire

The hearth fire with its magnetism, its warmth, light, hospitality and nurturing is, as it were, the Sun in miniature. We are all solar energised from the tiniest microbe to the largest mammal. All of us, of whatever species, are securely held in the intensely warm embrace of the Sun, which so selflessly expends itself in providing the energy for life: light, heat and nourishment.

The Sun is a million times larger than the Earth and all that takes place on Earth is made possible by the one billionth of the Sun's energy, which reaches it. If we were to pause for a moment to consider this awesome fact – all of life in every species in every age, all thought, activity, emotion, music, all movement and change is born of the Sun and made possible through the selfless gift of our lode-star.

Our foremothers and fathers had a profound reverence and respect for the Sun as they endeavoured to align themselves with the rising and setting Sun and Moon in an effort to achieve harmony of relationship with the divine cosmos. Who built the megaliths, the massive stone monuments dating back to 5,000 BCE? What was their purpose? Were these mysterious, sacred boulders used as dwellings, temples or tombs? In life and in death our ancestors were aware of the pivotal role of the Sun as evidenced by the widespread distribution of Stone Circles, Ring Forts and elaborate Chambered Cairns. These were normally erected to face the rising sun, for example passage tombs at Newgrange, Knowth, Dowth and Loughcrew in Co. Meath, Carrowmore and Carrowkeel in Co. Sligo and Court tombs, for example, Bavan and 'Temple of Deen' in Co. Donegal, Creevykeel in Co. Sligo and Browndod in Co. Antrim.

There are over a hundred portal tombs, mainly in the North and North-West and along a line from Dublin to

Waterford with Kilclooney in Co. Donegal and Legananny in
Co. Down providing elegant examples. There are some four
hundred wedge tombs known in Ireland, only a few have
been excavated, their distribution being mainly in the South
and South-West, particularly in Co. Clare, notably in the
Lough Gur area. Other notable examples are Toormore and
Island in Co. Cork, Moylisha in Co. Wicklow and
Baurnadomeeny in Co. Tipperary.[12]

The Grianan of Aileach is among the largest of the ancient
stone-built hill top enclosures in Ireland. It is closely related to
Staigue Fort in Co. Kerry, Dún Aenghus in Inishmore, Aran
Islands, Kilmurvey in Co. Clare and Doon Fort in Portnoo, Co.
Donegal. These were places of assembly rather than defensive
structures where people gathered for important ceremonies. In
Irish mythology, Grianan is regarded as an especially sacred
place. It stands on direct sun-wise rotation alignment
northwards with Uisneach, the centre or hearth of Ireland. A
little further along the same alignment northwards is Malin
Head, the most northerly point in Ireland, known as Banba's
Crown, thereby linking with Uisneach and the view of Ireland
as the living divinity, Ériu-Fodla-Banba. Grianan means
'sunhouse', which derives from 'grian', 'sun' and Grian, the sun
goddess. It was the home of Dagda, who is the supreme Sun
god of the earliest peoples of Ireland, rivalling Zeus of the
Greeks and Jupiter of the Romans and akin to the Christian
concept of God, the All-Knowing. Although the Dagda may
rule the universe he does not reign supreme:

> for within all ancient cosmologies the power of the
> Gods is confined within the limits of the 'Mother
> Goddess', who is not only the Earth but the Sun, the
> Moon and the very Heavens, the Creatrix, the All'. [13]

# Fire

The Grianan of Aileach guards the entrance to the Inishowen Peninsula between Lough Swilly and Lough Foyle and was the royal residence of the Ui Neill clan from the sixth to the twelfth century. The surrounding valley is home to several other early monuments notably the great stone circle at Beltaney, near Raphoe, which is the furthest west of the Stone Circles of Ulster. There are some 240 known stone circles in Ireland. Besides those in Ulster there is also a strong concentration in the Cork-Kerry area, in the east from Wicklow to Cavan and in the west from Lough Gur in Co. Limerick to the north Mayo coast.[14]

Several monuments honouring the mysteries of the universe and venerating the Sun characterise almost every place where our ancestors lived, for example Stonehenge, Carnac, shrines of Malta, Crete, Greece, Spain, parts of Asia, Africa, Australia, Cahokia Mounds in Illinois, USA together with the Inca, Mayan and Aztec treasures in Central and South America. There were the ceremonial celebrations surrounding the solstices and equinoxes as well as the cycles of the seasons of birth, growth, death and rebirth. The Sundance sacred ceremony among indigenous peoples is a striking example of the centrality of the Sun in our lives. Likewise Hindu chants in the holy river Ganges honouring the Sun and the festive summer celebrations in Nordic countries heralding the end of a long winter. In Iceland, for example, the word for light is 'ljós' and the word for midwife is 'ljósmódir', mother of light, the one who brings the new-born baby from the darkness of the womb into the light of the Sun.

Since time immemorial there has been a combination of wonder, fear, curiosity and superstition in our relationship with the celestial spheres. One of the most intriguing debates had been whether it is the Earth or the Sun that holds centre stage in the Solar System. Claudius Ptolemy placed the Earth in the centre with the Sun and other planets moving around it in circular orbits. This Earth-centred cosmology harmonised with the physics of Aristotle and dominated astronomical thought for fourteen centuries. A turning point came with the discoveries of Polish astronomer, Nicolas Copernicus (1473-1543). He argued that the Sun was stationary at the centre with the other planets moving around it in circular movements. Almost a century elapsed before Copernicus' idea was taken seriously when Johannes Kepler, a German (1571-1630), further observed that the planets do not move in perfect circles but in ellipses or elongated circles. However, it was not until Galileo Galilei, an Italian (1564-1642), who with the aid of his homemade telescopes recorded discoveries, which changed the whole direction of astronomy. He provided new evidence to enhance the Copernican revolution – the Sun is in the centre with the Earth and other planets orbiting it.

Copernicus' revolutionary insight, confirmed by Galileo, with regard to the movement of the heavenly spheres has, I believe, a deeper significance. What is it highlighting about us? Could it have been that promoting the Earth, as centre, was a euphemism for the human as centre of creation around which everything else orbited? The Sun is the centre, the real hearth that draws us in warmth, in sustenance, in play and in prayer. And furthermore we, as beings of all species, born of the Sun, which is a star, radiate this light, heat, energy, hospitality and nourishment. It is sobering to ponder if our hearth fire, the Sun, were to be extinguished that all life as we know it would cease. The hearth fire still burns in our interdependence and interrelatedness as species among species in the intricate and colourful tapestry of life. The fire of the Sun envelops the earth, water and air, energising them with life, but they are not consumed in the process. Likewise with us living beings, the fire of the Sun is the energy in our relationships.

When I go about growing food or shopping, when I take time to prepare and cook food together with family, friends or acquaintances, or perhaps alone, will I remember to acknowledge and celebrate the Sun, which is the key provider of the feast? When next I lie in the Sun, at home or abroad, and enjoy the warm touch of the sand and ocean waves, will I think of this free gift and thankfulness and remember to praise its Creator? When I take a brisk walk, cycle or exercise, when I work, plan, make deisions, when I sing, dance, write or paint, when I relax, pray or play will I even realise that the Sun is my constant companion, the breath, the energy, the life in me?

## Notes

1. Uranus was discovered in 1781, Neptune in 1846 and Pluto in 1930. For additional information see *Geographica, The Complete Illustrated Atlas of the World* Part 1 'Planet Earth', ed. Ray Hudson, (Random House, Australia, 1999).
2. H. Dorgan, D. Kennedy, S. Scott *The World of Science* 48, (Folens, Ireland, 1994).
3. Anne Primavesi *Gaia's Gift*, 9, (Routledge, London, 2003).
4. Brian Swimme & Thomas Berry *The Universe Story*, 148-9 (HarperSanFrancisco, 1992).
5. Cesair is a sun goddess, she is linked with the land of Ireland by the fresh-water umbilical cord of the three sister rivers: Barrow, Nore and Suir. Bith (meaning 'cosmos'), is her father. While fleeing floods with his family he reached Sliab Betha, Co. Fermanagh, where he drowned. He identified with the mountain, giving it his life, being, presence, it becomes the country's life-giving mountain.
6. Michael Dames *Mythic Ireland*, 196, (Thames and Hudson, London 1992).

7. Ibid. 208.
8. Brian Swimme *The Canticle to the Cosmos* 'The Primeval Fireball' Tape 11, The Tides Foundation (New Story Project, San Francisco, 1990).
9. Michael Dames *Mythic Ireland*, 208, (Thames and Hudson Ltd. London, 1992).
10. The Celtic seasons are: Samhain (Winter), Imbolc (Spring), Beltane (Summer), Lughnasadh (Autumn). For further reading see Caitlin Matthews *Celtic Devotional* (Gosfield Press, Great Britain, 1996).
11. The other seat of the High Kings was at Grianan of Aileach, Co. Donegal.
12. For further information on the Irish scene see Laurence Flanagan *Ancient Ireland, Life Before The Celts*, (Gill & Macmillan Ltd. Dublin, 1998).
13. Jack Roberts *The Sacred Mythological Centres of Ireland* 4, (Bandia, Ireland 1996, 1998, 2000).
14. For further reading see: Sean O'Nuallain *Stone Circles of Ireland*, (Country House, Dublin 1995), Michael Dames *Mythic Ireland*, (Thames and Hudson Ltd. London, 1992), Laurence Flanagan *Ancient Ireland*, (Gill & Macmillan, Dublin, 1998), Peter Harbison *Pre-Christian Ireland*, (Thames and Hudson Ltd., London 1998).

# OUT OF THE DANCE

## Emergence of the Earth and Early Life Forms

I dip my cupped hands. I drink
A long time. It tastes
like stone, leaves, fire. It falls cold
into my body, waking the bones. I hear them
deep inside me, whispering
oh what is that beautiful thing
that just happened?

> Mary Oliver
> from 'At Blackwater Pond'

Imagine a time before rocks and water or a time before forests
and grass. It is difficult to picture existence before colour and
fragrance, without birdsong, the buzz of insects or the vital
presence of plants, animals and people. Around 5 billion years
ago, life as we know it did not yet exist; planet Earth was
spinning in deep space as clumps of gas and dust orbiting the
newly-born Sun. Who could have predicted the amazing
variety and beauty of life forms that have continued to
emerge from that early cauldron? Every single being in the
community of creation was there, swirling, colliding and
dancing into distinct manifestations of the majestic universe

that birthed us. What an awesome thought – all of life, in every form, was potentially present at that beginning moment. Over the aeons that primal energy has been singing and shaping the countless manifestations of life. And the process continues. The words of the poet Carlyle come to mind: 'See deep enough and you see musically, the heart of nature being everywhere music, if you can only reach it'. Music is at the heart of it all inviting a rhythmic response. All of life is allured by the melody of the alchemist fashioning each one from the chemicals and minerals seeded in the original flaring forth almost 14 billion years ago. For some people this is the creative genius of God while others delight in the power and versatility of energy. Whatever our particular beliefs may be there is no doubt that life is absolutely amazing. Do we take time to stop in wonder, to gawk at the mystery all around us?

**Birthing of the Earth Within the Solar System**
It is not known precisely how Earth and its neighbouring planets were formed. We do know that they were formed at the same time and from the same substances and that there are significant differences between them. The most widely-held view is the so-called 'nebular theory' whereby the planets took shape from a disc of dust and gas that encircled the infant Sun. Another way of describing this is to think of the planets as formed in the afterbirth of the Sun, emerging as the placenta disintegrated in deep space. I like to image the Sun as the heartbeat of the Solar System, constantly radiating light, heat and energy to everything else that lives. This energy warms the Earth's surface, powers the wind and the waves, creates ocean currents and weather systems and recycles water. Sunlight is the basis of our food chain through

the miracle of photosynthesis. In this process, which began almost 4 billion years ago, plants learned to take nourishment from the Sun and initiated the cycle of mutual nourishment as species among species. What wisdom from the miracle of photosynthesis do we need to imbibe today? How might we live in a more mutually sustaining manner as the whole Earth community? A good place to begin is by getting to know the awesome story of who we are and how we came to be, of listening reverently to the voice of Earth, which birthed us all those aeons ago.

The Sun is the conductor *par excellence* of the magnificent symphony we call life, keeping all in tune and harmony in the dance of being. Earth enters the dance as one of the inner rocky planets orbiting the Sun and partnering Mercury, Venus and Mars. More gaseous partners, namely, Jupiter, Saturn, Uranus, Neptune and Pluto, surround these. The American writer, Henry David Thoreau, recognised and celebrated this privileged planet when he wrote:

> The Earth was the most glorious musical instrument and I was the audience to its strains.

What music brought forth the Earth and early life forms? What chords stirred in the primal fiery gases zooming in deep space, notes that would eventually sing your name and mine together with such haunting melodies as meadowsweet, sycamore, squirrel, kangaroo, cuckoo, salmon, butterfly, coral, Cherokee, Inishowen, Achill, Kilimanjaro, Niagara Falls, Alice Springs, Gullfoss, Amazon, Seychelles? Our ancestors told numerous stories about the origin of planet Earth within the larger Solar System in the Milky Way Galaxy. One such tale is the story of Sky Woman:

Once, the story goes a woman fell from the land in the sky. She fell through a hole made by the uprooting of a great tree and as she fell she grasped in her palm a handful of seeds. Down she fell, a long, long way. Below her there was no Earth, only the ancient waters and in those waters birds and animals swam.

'Look', they said, 'Someone is coming.'

Then some of the birds – Swans or Geese – flew up to catch her on their wings. Below, the other creatures held council.

'There must be a place for her to stand,' they said. 'We must bring up Earth'.

So, one after another, they dove down to try to bring up some mud from below that ancient sea. All of them failed but the last one – Muskrat. It brought up a tiny pawful of wet dirt.

'Now where shall we place it?' they said.

'Place it on my back,' a deep voice answered. It was the Great Turtle swimming up from the depths. When they placed the earth on Great Turtle's back it grew larger and larger until it became this continent on which we stand, this Earth on Great Turtle's back. There Sky Woman was placed by the birds. There she dropped the seeds, which grew into the good plants. So that story of Creation begins.[1]

## Out of the Dance

In a physical sense, the Earth, like the other planets, began as a very vast, dark and extremely hot cloud of gas and dust dancing around the newborn Sun. The pull of the Sun's gravity held all in its warm embrace as the spiral arm of the Milky Way Galaxy vibrated to the rhythm of the swirling

orbital journeys. Millions of years passed and the cloud of gas
and dust began to cool and condense into billions of droplets.
These were pulled together into clumps by their own
gravitational force. With the formation of one or more
clumps or boulders, sometimes colliding and scattering and
sometimes regrouping again, our planet Earth and the other
planets were born. However, it took another half billion years
for the Earth to cool sufficiently to form a solid crust and
sustain an atmosphere around it. The Earth is one of the
rocky inner planets in the Solar System with a core of nickel
and iron. Its rocky crust is composed largely of oxygen and
silicon. In fact the Earth is, as far as we know, the only planet
with the correct temperature at which water can exist on the
surface as well as being the only one containing oxygen.
Water and oxygen are both essential for life.

Is there life on Mars, the Red Planet, named after the
Roman god of war or Ares, his Greek counterpart? Today,
science suggests that water flowed across the planet's surface
at one time and that life might possibly have secured a
foothold. Research is ongoing and who knows but one day
we will discover Martian cousins. As the afterbirth of the
emerging Sun was transformed in space to form the planets –
there are others besides the nine we know of – who can state
categorically that only one possesses the exact elements and
combinations of chemicals to nurture life? Who can fathom
the mind of the Great Creator Spirit?

Earth is a cell of the Universe, which in its initial fiery
emergence all those billions of years ago produced the entire
body of chemicals, beginning with hydrogen and helium, the
lightest and most common. These basic components of the
Universe are also the basic components of the Earth itself and
in turn of all life. If I were to become totally present to and

gaze deeply within myself I would see the Sun, the rocks, the plants, I would taste the salt water, smell the sulphur, feel the wind and touch the mystery of at-one-ment with the entire community of creation. Without the basic life elements – hydrogen, oxygen, silicon, calcium, carbon and so forth I could not exist. We are intertwined, part of one another, we belong together in the creativity of divine genius. We have only to taste our tears to know where we come from. Curiously, the major religious traditions (with few exceptions), in placing the human above all beings in creation and in their sole emphasis on human life as sacred, have tried to extract the sacred from the other than human elements from which life emerged. Is there not the risk of tampering with what is ultimately mystery and deciding how God ought to behave? Can the Creator fashion anything that is not sacred and therefore worthy of reverence and respect?

> Where were you when I laid the foundation of the earth? Tell me, if you have understanding. Who determined its measurements – surely you know! Or who stretched the line upon it? On what were its bases sunk, or who laid its cornerstone when the morning stars sang together and all the heavenly beings shouted for joy?[2]

### Earth: One System, a Model Recycler

The story of the evolutionary journey of Earth over the past four and a half billion years is a manifestation of a living system in harmony with the larger Universe system. The Earth is, as it were, a sub-system of the living universe system. Our human systems – education, health, justice, religion, economics and politics – are sub-systems of the living organism, planet Earth. The challenge is for us to try to align our systems with the Earth system rather than create parallel or counter systems. We do the latter most blatantly when we persist in living apart from or superior to all other beings in the total community of life. Our systems, whether education, health, politics, economics, justice or religion have become entirely human-centred and orientated to the exclusion of all other species. The devastating effects of such a way of thinking and living are all around us. Let us wake up and open all our senses before it is too late.

The conservation of energy and the recycling of finite resources are values intrinsic to Earth in its origin, evolution and direction. The three major recycling systems, which characterise Earth from its beginnings, are: the lithosphere (rock sphere), the hydrosphere (water sphere) and the atmosphere (gaseous envelope surrounding the Earth).

> Almost no rock on the surface of the Earth today is original rock. Even granite almost four billion years old has already been recycled.[3]

Water evaporates, rises, cools and falls as rain in the hydrological cycle. The Sun powers the circulation of water on planet Earth. The sun's rays heat the surface of the oceans, causing water to evaporate. This accounts for some 90 per cent of the water in the atmosphere; the remainder comes from moisture evaporating from rivers, lakes, wet soil and the respiration of plants and animals. The heat in the evaporation process, forming water vapour, cools as it rises. Water vapour forms clouds, which deposit moisture in the form of rain or snow, back to the surface of the Earth. The water, when it falls as rain or snow, renders the atmosphere a little warmer. Thus the heat of evaporation is carried from the sea to the atmosphere making the surface layer of the oceans a veritable storage heater that helps to improve the climactic conditions of adjacent landmasses.

Other organisms in the community of life have already recycled the air that I breathe at this moment. It is legitimate to say that the air filling my lungs at any moment may well have been exhaled by the song thrush nearby, by the cheetah gracing the African plains or the birthing or perhaps dying breath of people in my neighbourhood. That same air recycled over the millennia links us across the generations. The Earth breathes in us and we unite in a sort of universal breath of life. The operation of Earth as a cohesive system teaches us the absolute preciousness of resources and the secret of optimum use and minimum wastage. The language of Earth is a vocabulary resounding in conservation and care. Whatever dies comes to life again, as we know from observing the rhythms of the seasons. If only we could heed this wisdom particularly in our growing affluent and 'throw-away' lifestyles. Let us listen to the whisperings of the ancient elements birthing the Earth in order to be challenged anew to live in a more mutually enhancing and sustainable way as one community of life.

## Rock and Roll
The story of the Earth is an epic, a remarkable account of life emerging. This wonderful story takes us from inhospitable beginnings, when Earth was a place of some 80 per cent carbon dioxide with no free oxygen, to an alive and self-sustaining place, which is our home today. The early form was homogeneous, a mixture of silicates and metals. Through the differentiation process three stages emerged. Iron and

nickel collected at the centre to form the inner core. Then some of the metals, including oxygen, combined with the silicates to create a surrounding mantle. It was then left to the lighter materials to solidify and form an outer crust. The deep inner core of the Earth is solid with an outer fluid zone of concentric layers, which are covered by the mantle. This is a thick layer of molten rock about 2800 kilometres deep. The upper mantle and solid outer crust, called the lithosphere, is about thirty-five to forty kilometres thick beneath the continents, thicker still under larger mountain ranges and dwindling to six kilometres thick under the oceans.

The crust may be likened to the skin that forms on rice pudding as it cools. It forms the land and ocean floor covering a mantle of molten rock, hot seething and ever ready to erupt on to the surface in volcanic ferocity and blazing glory. The Earth's crust is made up of a number of sections or plates, some minor and some major, which fit together like a massive jigsaw puzzle. These plates are constantly moving or drifting on the mantle; this is known as 'continental drift'. The annual rate of movement can be as little as 1.3 cm or as much as 10 cm. If the plates or rock-shafts collide, one edge could be forced either upwards to form mountain ranges or downwards to create ocean depths. This process is known as 'plate tectonics'. About 200 million years ago all land masses on the Earth were joined together forming a super-continent, named Pangaea, an ancient Greek term meaning 'whole earth'. Pangaea was surrounded by one vast ocean called Panthalassa. Slowly, with the process of plate movement, the continents began to drift apart forming the great oceans and finally about 65,000 years ago forming the patterns familiar to us today. Our continental landmasses are still moving but very, very slowly. North America is moving away from

Eurasia at the rate of about three centimetres per year, while the Pacific Ocean is shrinking in size.

In his book, *Where Has Ireland Come From?*,' Frank Mitchell traces the fascinating geological story of Ireland's journey over the past 500 million years from some 30 degrees south of the equator to our present location between 51.5-55.5 degrees north latitude. Prior to 500 million years ago Ireland was in two distinct parts separated by an early Atlantic Ocean. This phase ended with the coming together of the American and European plates forming a great plane. The welding together of the two parts of the island of Ireland was along a line running from Clogherhead on the east coast north of Drogheda and Galway Bay on the west coast. This united plate remained in southern latitudes at approximately the level of South Africa for about a million years. During the succeeding 400 million years Ireland was ferried slowly northwards as plates jostled and danced, raising up mountains and razing them to the ground, carving out the ocean depths and the surface contours of planet Earth. Over the 9000 kilometres trek northwards the Irish landscape has witnessed monumental changes. It has been submerged beneath the sea, donned the desert mantle, sported ice caps and danced in tropical forest attire before finally relaxing into the mild, moist green of temperate zones. And, however unlikely it may seem to us, our rock mass has experienced earthquakes and volcanic eruptions during its long history.

There are three different types of rocks on planet Earth; igneous, sedimentary and metamorphic. Rocks combine a variety of minerals. These are inorganic substances with clear atomic and chemical structures. Igneous, from the Latin *'ignis'*, 'fire', describes rocks formed when hot molten material, or magma, welling up from beneath the Earth's crust solidifies. Basalt and granite are common types of igneous rock.

Sedimentary rocks are formed from material deposited by wind and water. As the layers pile up the sediment is squeezed into rock, that is, sand becomes sandstone and mud is compressed into clay. These rocks include limestone, chalk, shale, sandstone and coal. Metamorphic rocks are rocks that have undergone change from the existing igneous or sedimentary types, for example limestone becomes marble, granite become gneiss and sandstone becomes quartzite. The recycling of rock minerals ensures a connection between the different kinds of rock configuring the Earth's surface.

When I think of these different rock formations, the echoes of primal stars, I wonder about our deep connections. Like the rocks I am born of stardust. I too have rumbled in the womb of Earth before coming forth into the light. What is the igneous activity in my life, where is the fire? What solid ground does my fiery passion create so that life may abound? Does my hospitality for all beings radiate from an inner warmth born of the stars from which we all emerged? The sedimentary rocks speak to me of layers, my genetic coding, cultural coding, ethnic, socio-economic, political and religious traditions. What presses me into shape? Where do I need to loosen up and what needs to erode? Metamorphic rocks exude the freedom to change. How open am I to the ebb and flow of life's transforming influence? What perceptions, ideas, beliefs, attitudes yearn for expansion?

There is a sense in which it is true to say that Earth is in its element when dancing in rocks, air, water and fire. Volcanoes occur where the fiery liquid rock beneath the surface sizzles through cracks in the Earth's crust before spewing out as lava or magma spilling over the surrounding area. Lava, rock and ash build up to form a mountain with a crater on top. Most volcanic activity occurs where two rock plates are pushing against one another or moving apart. Many of the world's active volcanoes are found in an area around the Pacific Ocean, known as the 'Pacific Ring of Fire'. Volcanic eruptions are mostly under the sea. Deep under the Atlantic Ocean where the North American Plate is pulling away from the Eurasian Plate, molten magma (liquid rock) fissures up to fill the gap between the plates. This lava eventually cools and solidifies to form new land. Over time this process created a vast mountain range, known as the Mid-Atlantic Ridge. These mountains formed of volcanic rock rise thousands of metres from the ocean floor and some rise above sea level to create islands. Iceland is one such creation. Volcanic activity is so much part of Icelandic life that the people use this resource to heat water for their homes, outdoor swimming pools, health spas and sulphur baths. Krafla, Hekla on the mainland and Heimaey on the Westmann Islands (named after the Irish slaves of Viking raids) to the south of the Island are among the most active volcanoes.

In 1963 the island of Surtsey was spewed up from the bowels of the Earth and appeared near Iceland after almost a month rising from the waves. In Italy, Vesuvius erupted in 79 CE burying the city of Pompeii whose ruins were not discovered until 1748. Pompeii, about five miles from Vesuvius, was buried under ten feet of ash by the ferocious eruption. People, plants and animals were solidified where they were at that awful moment. Poisonous fumes killed a further two thousand people. It is still an active volcano. Hot springs and geysers occur when fiery rocks beneath the Earth's surface heat underground water. This boiling water then rises up and steams its way through cracks in the ground. A geyser is a natural fountain heated under severe pressure, which spouts water and steam at regular intervals. Yellowstone Park in Wyoming, USA, is home to many geysers, including one nicknamed 'Old Faithful'. New Zealand and Iceland (from where the name originates) are other notable areas of geyser activity.

Tectonic plates of the Earth's crust usually move slowly; however, they sometimes collide causing deep cracks in the rock called fault lines. They do this with enormous force setting up vibrations somewhat like the noise of crashing stones only magnified. These massive vibrations are earthquakes, the Earth literally shudders, often provoking terror and causing great damage. Most earthquakes occur around the edges of the Pacific Ocean or close to dense mountainous areas like the Himalayas on the Indian subcontinent. The Tokyo earthquake in Japan in 1923 caused the most damage to the environment and to humans in modern times followed by the more recent El Salvador disaster during which thousands of people perished or became homeless. In December 2003 over forty thousand people were killed when the ancient city of Bam in Southern Iran was hit by an earthquake. Many earthquakes occur within the oceans and only a fraction of all earthquakes are experienced directly by people. Submarine earthquakes can cause massive fast-moving ocean waves called 'tsunamis', or tidal waves, which are capable of scaling heights of up to ten metres. A notable example of this powerful and deadly movement is the 1775 earthquake in Lisbon, Portugal, which created a tsunami killing several thousand people in a little over one minute. Apart from these violent and devastating Earth movements there are lesser tremors experienced by many people. In such conditions one does not need to be reminded that the Earth is moving, however slowly, and what seems still is in constant flux. The 'rock 'n' roll' dance of life continues, it is the style and tempo that vary from time to time.

## Riverdance

Earth's choreography is by no means confined to volcanic and tectonic movements alone. Weather patterns and climactic conditions add their special touch to the dance of life. The Sun heats up the great oceans and waterways across the globe causing water to evaporate and rise upward. The higher it rises the colder it gets, forming an invisible gas called water vapour. When water vapour cools it forms liquid droplets, which come together to form clouds and eventually, as these grow heavier, they fall as rain back into the oceans and landmasses. The water cycle, also known as the hydrological cycle, is nature's way of recycling; existing water is recycled again and again making it a renewable resource. Would that we humans, especially in the Western world, could heed this example! Less than 1 per cent of the total mass of water is held in rivers, lakes, the atmosphere, rocks and soil, about 97 per cent is stored in the oceans as salt water while the remainder (approximately 2 per cent) is frozen as snow and ice.

## Twist and Shake

Life on planet Earth is made possible by the atmosphere, a blanket of air that provides a dome-like protection, warmth and most importantly the oxygen we need to breathe and live. The atmosphere is made up of 77 per cent nitrogen, 21 per cent oxygen and 2 per cent other gases, for example, water vapour. The atmosphere has several identifiable layers, the one perhaps most familiar to us being the ozone layer. About 30 kilometres (19 miles) above the Earth's surface is the ozone layer, created by potentially deadly ultraviolet radiation from the Sun striking oxygen in the stratosphere. The ozone layer protects life on Earth from these harmful ultraviolet rays. We humans are progressively upsetting this atmospheric dance of life by our over-consumption of fossil fuels and carbon monoxide emissions from cars, buses, lorries, and sea and air transport, in addition to over stocking of cattle to satiate burger-hungry outlets. All these factors together contribute alarming amounts of methane gas to an already fragile atmospheric protective covering.

The movement of air and the dance of air masses bring weather changes, which are also affected by seasonal patterns. Weather affects how we live and where we live, as well as what we eat, wear and even our leisure activities. Sometimes weather conditions can be powerful and dramatic as in thunderstorms, hurricanes and tornadoes. Thunderstorms occur when warm, humid air rises rapidly forming massive cumulonimbus storm clouds. Inside these clouds tiny water droplets and ice crystals whirl around colliding and sparking off one another and creating tiny electrical charges in the process. Gradually these sparks become giant flashes from cloud to cloud or to the ground and back. There are literally thousands of thunderstorms every day most of which can be as explosive as an atom bomb. Tornadoes are violently rotating wind-storms with winds gusting up to 800 kilometres per hour. These devastating, funnel-shaped clouds, often called 'twisters', occur mainly on the plains of North America and can lift houses and machinery as they leapfrog across the land. Hurricanes, typhoons or cyclones are powerful and devastating tropical storms occurring mainly in late summer and early autumn. They are fuelled by thousands of tonnes of rain and strong gales encircling a clear, calm patch at the centre, called the eye. That can inflict a great deal of damage as they reach land as evidenced from recent incidents in, for example, the Caribbean, Florida, India, Bangladesh, Hawaii and the Philippines.

The often frenzied dance of nature and the forces at work within and around planet Earth have intrigued people from the beginning. The Chinese of ancient times believed that storms were the result of dragons battling in the sky, breathing fire and destruction. Many peoples worshipped goddesses and gods of fire, of sea, of sky and of earth. The early Egyptians worshipped Nut, who was a sky goddess and twin sister of the earth goddess Geb. For some, volcanic eruptions signified the ire of the gods; these fire mountains summoned them to repentance. Poseidon was the Greek god of the sea, the equivalent of the Roman god Neptune. He rode the ocean waves in a chariot and with his powerful three-pronged trident 'shattered the rocks, called forth storms and shook the earth'.[5]

## Into the Dance – Early Life Forms

The rhythm of the lithosphere, the hydrosphere and the atmosphere in swirling movement evoked the emergence of life in the biosphere. This is the space linking the ocean floor to the sky, which today is home to a large and varied community of life. One way of imagining this is to view the infant Earth as a giant cauldron of pre-biotic soup stirring in space. How did life in its myriad forms emerge from this richly flavoured, boiling hot and well-seasoned stock? It has to be acknowledged that nobody knows for certain, but with the aid of ever more penetrating and precise telescopes and microscopes, carbon dating, fossil reading, exploration of ocean depths, forest canopies and polar ice we are able to shape the jigsaw more accurately and comprehensively.

# Dance

All living things, or organisms, are composed of cells. These tiny units of self-contained molecules are the building blocks of life with powers of duplication from generation to generation. The history of Earth's early life forms, known as 'biota', can be deduced by scientists from physical evidence such as rock fossils together with biochemical data. The Grand Canyon in western United States exhibits the deepest cleft that exists on the surface of the Earth. This is a precious area for fossil data extending backwards for thousands of years. The Atlas Mountains of Morocco in northern Africa are even older in their preservation of fossil remains, particularly of the invertebrates (organisms without backbone). The tropical forest areas of the world, particularly of the Great Amazon Basin in South America, together with the Great Barrier Reef, extending for over a thousand miles and running parallel to the eastern coast of Australia, are special areas of ancestral information in the community of life.

What was the synthesis that sparked the first flicker of life? In the elemental mixture of earth, air, water and fire of the Sun were many elements. Four of these were destined to be essential for life, namely, oxygen and hydrogen (constituents of water), and carbon and nitrogen (present in the atmosphere). In order to transform these into life a transfusion of energy was required. Where might this have come from? One can only imagine the creativity and effort upon effort as the young, gregarious Earth teetered on the brink of a new and exciting phase in its development. How many miscarriages were there? We will never know. The absolute mystery of it all evokes awe and wonder and even surprise. The gift of life for each of us individually and for the community of life as a whole is so precious, delicately balanced and complex:

Sun and Earth awakened Earth's life. The energy of the
solar system transformed atmosphere and ocean,
swirled into young seething Earth and erupted as
lightening that initiated the proto-cellular chemical
reactions. Life here was born in a lightning flash. Earth's
life is lightning embodied and made flesh.[6]

Another possible locus of synthesis was in the depths of the
oceans where the accumulation of salt and pressure could
have created the life-giving impetus. A further radical
alternative proposal about the origins of life was initially
put forward by German biologist Herman von Helmholtz
in 1847 and revived by Sir Fred Hoyle and Professor
Chandra Wickramasinghe in the 1970s. This is known as
'panspermia' (from Greek meaning 'life everywhere'), and
proposes that life was seeded on planet Earth from
elsewhere in the cosmos. They claim that life on Earth
emerged as a result of comets colliding with planets and
thereby seeding them with bacterial life in the early stages
of the Solar System. Could the claim that bacteria,
constantly swirling in space and falling to Earth from the
vast, interstellar dust and gas clouds – freeze-dried bacteria
– seeded the earth be substantiated? We will have to wait
and see the outcome of further scientific evidence of what
is an exciting proposition.[7]

Whatever the decisive spark, it appears that 4 billion
years ago the latent self-organising dynamics, which
characterise the universe at every level, were evoked. The
moment had arrived for Earth to proclaim itself in a whole
new way. The chemical mix of carbohydrates, fats and
proteins was present in the oceans birthing the first simple
organisms (organised life chemicals).

# Dance

The first life-forms consist of single-celled archaebacteria, known as 'prokaryotes'. These early creatures have no nucleus – 'prokaryote' means 'before nucleus or kernel' – and their internal structure is less specialised than later, more complex, organisms. These are the most vital form of life on planet Earth, if they were to be eliminated, all life would cease. There are about ten thousand species of protistans, most of which are invisible to the naked eye.

The earliest forms may be likened to the bacteria-like organisms inhabiting hot springs associated with volcanic activity today. The only source of energy available to these early organisms was that found on the water floating around them and this was in short supply. However, in this moment of crisis, the muscles of life were flexed in creativity. A new life chemical was created, a green pigment called the chlorophyll molecule – the miracle of photosynthesis, which changed the planet. Swirling in their ocean habitat creatures learned to take nourishment from the Sun, thereby initiating the process of mutual nourishment within the fledgling community of life. By absorbing solar energy together with organic matter from Earth and possibly matter from outer space through comets and asteroids, these 'pre-life' forms became increasingly complex. Mysteriously they transformed into living cells.

About 1.8 billion years ago a crisis arose when the prokaryotes were causing an oxygen surplus. This was like a lethal acid in the atmosphere. Evolutionary creativity came to the rescue once more. Mitochondria evolved; these bacteria could deal with oxygen so they entered into a relationship with existing bacteria, the deal being nourishment. In their book, *A Walk Through Time*, authors Liebes, Sahtouris and Swimme capture the benefits of community life for the early microbes:

Microbial mats form richly layered ecosystems, and under the right conditions, these become stromatolite bacterial skyscrapers. The blue-greens live in the top layers, slipping in and out of UV-light – shielding sheaths to gather solar energy. Cyanobacteria produce prodigious amounts of food. 'Consumer' bacteria, immune to oxygen, quickly join the cyanobacteria. Beneath them live mixed populations of consumers and producers, each possessing unique diets and tolerances for oxygen, light and sulfides.[8]

Both the ancient bacteria and those that photosynthesise are single-celled organisms that lack a nucleus and whose DNA is not grouped into chromosomes.[9] All other life forms of planet Earth are characterised by more structured cells with a nucleus and chromosomes. These organisms are called 'eukaryotes' and they are responsible for all the more complex forms of life. In the prokaryote community, photosynthesis and the development of mitochondria (oxygen burners) created the identity. These early organisms reproduced asexually, they simply divided to create exact copies of themselves. Bacteria are immortal, that is, provided the environmental factors are right. They may, however, be killed by outside predators, for example, chlorofluorocarbons (CFCs) or terrorist-like antibiotics.

Multi-cellular organisms manifested by plants some 1.3 billion years ago were a major step on the evolutionary journey. Through gathering together, cells discovered that their survival was greatly enhanced. This was followed about one billion years ago by sexuality. All reproduction is by cell division, but sexual reproduction heralded almost infinite possibilities. The offspring inherits one set of chromosomes from each parent. Since each may be beneficial in a different environment the chances of survival are more secure. The astonishing diversity of life present from the beginning becomes ever more obvious through the mode of inheritance. Physical characteristics, or genes, are passed intact from parent to offspring, some appearing in each generation while others are recessive. It is now known that genes form strands called chromosomes inside the cell nucleus. The genes occur in pairs and the strands in matching sets, with each set containing a basic number of chromosomes. Chromosomes are long spiralling threads of DNA molecules:

> Life is an activation of something that is pervasive in the universe. Its dynamics can form only certain kinds of compounds. One kind is nucleic acid. The nucleic acids are fundamental to the DNA.[10]

DNA is a chemical compound made up of nitrogen, sugar and phosphate. It most likely evolved during the early period of the ancient bacteria (archean), as a mutation of RNA (ribonucleic acid). This nucleic acid single strand is operative in the transfer of messages of DNA and the flow of amino acids, which are essential in the development of life. When the DNA activates amino acids it unzips and replicates, this is known as the genetic code. This genetic code is the language of all life forms and for us humans precedes our cultural coding. Which do we value most? Which do we listen to in our policy and decision-making, one or both? The genetic language code is the music of the rocks, the dance of life, the song of the universe, the silence of mystery.

Carbohydrates, fats and proteins, these form the stuff of life; chlorophyll is the transformer of light into living energy; and DNA is the substance with the long memory that is able to store and, with help, replicate the information of life. This was the package deal of chemical evolution, a do-it-itself kit that was to transform the non-living world into a living one.[11]

With sexuality came death: death has the power to terminate biological forms and to create the possibility for new genetic forms. In his explanation of the story of life, Brian Swimme, tells us that:

For life forms that are sexual, death is part of their unfolding. It is worked into the organism. The early bacteria could actually avoid death. It is possible that some of the earliest bacteria are still with us today.[12]

Early life continued evolving in the oceans. Among the more primitive creatures are the sponges, jellyfish, sea anemones and corals. The life forms that evolved after these right up until the more advanced backbone and nervous system variety, that is, before 700 million years ago, can be classified as: shelled animals (trilobites, clams, sea snails), symmetrical creatures (starfish, sea urchins), and animals with segmented bodies that are elongated in form (wriggling worms, lobsters, shrimps).[13] Worms were the first creatures to possess brains and nervous system c. 670 million years ago.

## The Backbone of the Universe
The magnificence of divine creativity took on a whole new manifestation some 500 million years ago with the

development of the vertebrates (organisms with a backbone). The first fish forms with backbone emerged, protecting the Earth's earliest and most delicate nervous system and the development of its sensory organs. I like to think of fish as the literature of the oceans opening up for us a school of insight and knowledge born out of imbibed ancient wisdom and imaginative leaping forward. Endowed with a wonderful skeletal design, well-developed brain, organs, muscles and glands, they enjoy freedom of movement and independence hitherto unknown as they dance through the restless waters. They are the birds of the sea, fin-propelled, gliding, darting in self-defence, migrating, mating in ritual dance, laying eggs and nurturing their young. In a real sense theirs is the melody, the music accompaniment of the swansong to our existence in the seas, the fanfare marking our coming ashore 424 million years ago.

Can we abandon our ocean home? Is it possible to ignore the womb that bore us, that nourished us in the past and continues in umbilical intimacy to water our growth and development? Water is essential for life. There is but one ocean flowing through all of creation, circulating in my veins, in my tears of laughter and sorrow, watering my hopes, dreams, choices, ideas, plans, decisions and bridging the flow of unity and interconnectedness in the sacred community of life. Water is more than the fusion of hydrogen and oxygen, it is the stuff of life, it is sentiment, it is poetry, it is mystery. What kind of insanity would lead me to destroy, pollute, waste or take for granted this lifeline? According to a recent UNDP Report close to 2 billion people lack access to safe drinking water, 3 billion are without proper sanitation facilities and clean water is lacking in over eighty countries.[14] As the community of life, water is in our very bones, in damaging it we are rendering the fabric of existence brittle and vulnerable. Mary Oliver, an American nature poet, celebrates this profound bonding in the following extract from her poem called 'The Sea':[15]

Stroke by
    stroke my
        body remembers that life and cries for
            the lost parts of itself –
                fins, gills
                    opening like flowers into
the flesh – my legs
    want to lock and become
        one muscle, I swear I know
            just what the blue-gray scales
                shingling the rest of me
                    would feel like!

## Notes

1. Quoted in *The Way of the Earth*, 435-6, by T.C. McLuhan, (Simon & Schuster, New York, London, Toronto, Sydney, Tokyo, Singapore, 1994).
2. Job 38:4-7 *The Bible: New Revised Standard Version* (American Bible Society, New York, 1989).
3. *A Walk Through Time, From Stardust to Us* Sidney Liebes, Elisabet Sahtouris, Brian Swimme, 29, (John Wiley & Sons Inc., New York Toronto, Singapore, 1998).
4. *Where Has Ireland Come From?* Frank Mitchell, 5-10, (Town House and Country House, Dublin, 1994). Reprinted in 2000
5. Quoted in *The Ultimate Encyclopedia of Mythology* eds., Cotterell & R. Storm, 76, (Lorenz Books, 1999) 76.
6. *The Universe Story*, eds., Brian Swimme & Thomas Berry, 86 (Harper SanFrancisco, 1994).

7. *Science Today*, 'Life from outer Space' by Dr William Reville the *Irish Times* 15 November, 2001.
8. *A Walk Through Time*, eds., S. Liebes, E. Sahtouris & B. Swimme, 38, (John Wiley & Sons, Inc. New York, Chicester, Weinheim, Brisbane Singapore, Toronto, 1998).
9. DNA, deoxyribonucleic acid, is a substance present in the cell nuclei of nearly all living organisms. It is the main constituent of chromosomes, the carrier of genetic information.
10. *Canticle To the Cosmos* Tape Seven 'Sex, Death, and Dreams' by Brian Swimme 1990, (New Story Project, Tides Foundation, San Francisco CA).
11. *The Life-Giving Sea*, David Bellamy, 37, (Hamish Hamilton, London, 1975).
12. *Canticle To The Cosmos*.
13. For a more comprehensive account of the story of life see *Life on Earth* by David Attenborough (Fontana Press, British Broadcasting Corporation, 1979).
14. UNDP, United Nations, New York, 1998.
15. Mary Oliver *New and Selected Poems*, 172, (Beacon Press, Boston, 1992).

# Out Of The Waters

## Life Comes Ashore – Profuse and Diverse

> The disciples asked, 'When will the kingdom come?'
> Jesus replied, 'The kingdom will not come by expectation.
> Nor will it do to say, "Here it is" or "There it is"!
> Rather the kingdom of heaven is spread out on Earth,
> But people do not see it.'
> Gospel of Thomas

Life was born in the oceans. As living beings more than 90 per cent of our existence has been solely in the seas. This is difficult to absorb. One evening in summer as I strolled on Culdaff Beach in Donegal, I was mesmerised by the ebb and flow of the evening tide. I began to ponder the ebb and flow of my own life and almost like entering a trance I became deeply attuned to the rhythm of the waves as their music spilled around my feet, cool and refreshing. I fingered the sand remodelled by footsteps and tracks from the day's heat and thought 'you were once rock'. And so am I – born of stardust, from boulders of dust and gas swirling in the early universe emerging from the Godhead:

In each of us, three million potassium atoms explode every minute – far-reaching remnants of the supernova

explosion that gave birth to our solar system —
reminders that we are truly stardust.[1]

Transfixed at the water's edge I could feel myself swirling in
the waters with our earliest ancestors in the community of
life, the soothing water flowing through my veins deep in
the womb of the oceans. At that moment I shared the
experience of the poet Rilke: 'I feel closer to what language
cannot reach'.[2] The water was like a gigantic mirror
reflecting crumpled images of time and eternity. There is a
stirring sense of reality when one remains still and ankle-
deep at water's edge. In those moments I catch a glimpse of
what it means to be in constant cosmic rhythm even
though I appear to be standing still. Here the invisible and
visible embrace.

There was an intimacy that evening on the beach, a
sense of belonging. To be is to long, to yearn for a sense of
relationship, of purpose, of meaning and a sense of place. I
thought of togetherness. Communing. I tried to imagine a
time before water. What foresight brought together the
creativity of hydrogen and oxygen in the first instance?
Out of that union water was created and continues to
nurture life in all its magnificence. The music of the waves
spoke to me of memories. There were cosmic memories of
aeons of life, of change, movement and evolutionary
journeys all rolled up and glittering in the purple-pink glow
of the fading Sun behind the sand dunes. As the waves
swelled onto the now deserted beach I had the sensation of
being enveloped by the presence of billions of creatures.
They seemed to be echoing down through the ages,
whispering secrets of togetherness long since forgotten in
so many regions of our twenty-first century world.

I felt the urge to enter into the waves, to mingle with the guests of life in swirling familiarity. Though I am a creature of habit in terms of swimming, I was even prepared to forego the luxury of having the Sun blazing overhead before I could ever dream of sensing the water above my ankles. In haste I prepared for the plunge, wading in and easing into the cushion of life that had cradled me for billions of years. Relaxing in the buoyancy of the salty waters I recalled the story of the Salt Doll.[3] This is a tale about a salt doll who, having journeyed for thousands of miles over land, came upon a strange moving mass. This was quite different to anything she had seen before. She became curious and asked: 'Who are you?' The sea smiled and replied 'Come in and see.' She began to wade in, deeper and deeper until only a tiny piece remained. In that moment she discovered her true identity, at one with the mighty ocean. This was a defining moment for me. I am who I am in relationship. To be in isolation is impossible. The tingling of the water against my skin was expanding my consciousness. It is the same water since the beginning recycled time and time again relaying the secrets of connectedness across time and eternity and embracing all created reality. Here is home.

I lay back in the secure lap of the ocean. What mysteries were lapping around me, what stories riding the waves? There was an overwhelming sense of place, of awe and wonderment. How amazing is creation. How wonderful is my birth, the birth of all creatures. I slowly began to unravel the strands of life. There is the interconnecting of chemicals and minerals, wind and waves, of rocks and Sun giving of themselves in weathering, polishing, refining, in preparing life for more and more stupendous manifestations of itself. We are earthlings among the extended family of earthlings in the community we call the universe. What does this mean? Let's take the image of story. I think of story as the art of enchantment by the real and the imaginary, where these two are not separate, but intertwined in search of meaning. Each of us are storied beings, we have our personal, family, ethnic, cultural, political, socio-economic and, for many, a religious story. We have a cosmic story too, hitherto for the most part little understood or acknowledged.

## Story of Stories

The cosmic identity, our genesis or origin story, expands all our other stories and holds them in their integrity and in context. It is all-inclusive. Whatever my gender, ethnic identity, sexual orientation, political or religious affiliation, I belong in the cosmic story. Our cosmic story is more than 13 billion years old, it is the longest story ever told and is still evolving: 'the only text without a context' as Thomas Berry reminds us. Each one of us is actively involved in this unfolding, telling the story in our own unique manner simply by being who we are in the community of life. What a chorus! Can we allow ourselves the delight of hearing it and more profoundly of tuning in and becoming part of it, the community of life in prayer, praising the Great Spirit, the Creator? Mechtild of Magdeburg, one of the medieval mystics, expressed it thus:

> The day of my spiritual awakening was the day I saw – and knew I saw – all things in God and God in all things.[4]

## A Whole New Adventure

Deep within the primal waters teeming with life there were early rumblings of something new emerging. The plants were on the move, the first to land. They came ashore over 400 million years ago and slowly explored their new habitat around the continents. These early pioneers were probably similar to modern mosses, lichens and liverworts. Was this a sense of adventure or was it an effort to escape predators and overcrowding in the oceans? I try to imagine the bravery involved in this giant step.

Recycling is an essential element in the process of life. The oceans at this time were teeming with recycling organisms. Dead multi-celled creatures provide the staple diet for microbes, which are the prime recyclers. The first life form to leave the oceans, the wood cell, had developed a membrane within which it could carry its own water supply. The landscape must have resembled the pictures we see from space, particularly the lunar terrain with its seemingly endless tracts of barren, baked rocks, dust and debris. No soil covering, no green, no flowers or trees, no birdsong or butterflies. There was the arid heat, the leaving behind of the warm and comfortable cocoon of water and companionship of ocean communities. And there was gravity, a force unknown in the watery depths. Who survived? How many perished in this courageous adventure? We can only surmise.

Every new breakthrough in the divine creativity evokes multiple possibilities. Within these early algae and fledgling plants inventiveness was at work, creating the wood cell, which could withstand the crushing and disorienting power of gravity. The wood cell may have evolved from semi-aquatic plants struggling to survive at the water's edge. These battled with the force of gravity as water ebbed and flowed or as water levels swelled or dried up over millions of years. Fungi – mushrooms, yeasts – also appear on the shores. Fungi reproduce in two ways, sexually and by way of spores. Plants and fungi are closely associated. Fungi are recyclers. They get their food by breaking down the tissues of both living and dead plants and animals. There are some 70,000 known species of fungus, some helpful and some poisonous. Among the former are yeasts used in bread, beer and wine-making. Other types of fungus produce penicillin and antibiotics helpful to human and animal life.

### Swarming Colonisers
The spread of plants was soon followed by the arrival of animals on dry land. The first animals to emerge from the waters were arthropods, probably millipedes. These invertebrate animals had a segmented body with an external skeleton and jointed limbs. They formed an interdependent community with land plants. Among the earliest insects to come ashore were cockroaches and dragonflies. They learned to adapt to new worlds. Insects inhabit all corners, swimming below the water, swarming in forests and arid deserts, crawling in bright sunlight and in the dark recesses of the planet. They can soar over the highest peaks, live in ice-caps or dwell in hot, volcanic pools. A single tree can be literally 'crawling' with insects, some among the roots, some on or under the bark and some on the leaves. Some seek a home deep in animal flesh or snuggle within the thickness of a leaf. Some construct veritable fortresses (Australian compass termites) while others build massive hills (ants, termites).

Insects are the most numerous, outnumbering by as much as three times all other kinds of animal put together. In fact, it is impossible to determine the number of individual insects, but a fair guess would reckon that every human being alive has some million or so of them as companions! They bring music and colour to our lives as well as being essential in the nourishing and healing processes of the communities of life. Relatively speaking, insects are among the most feared in the animal population. They colonised the land before the arrival of the vertebrates and they continue to make their presence felt in all sorts of ways. Humans have battled with insects for centuries because of their bloodsucking instinct, their stings, bites and their propensity to spread disease but to little avail, as David Attenborough reminds us:

> He [human] synthesises new chemical poisons of the most lethal kind and sprays the countryside wholesale. And yet, in spite of all his efforts and ingenuity, of huge expenditures of labour and money, he has so far failed to exterminate a single species.[5]

Chief Dan George (1899-1981), hereditary chief of the Coast Salish tribe, British Columbia, offers an alternative view from the indigenous peoples' sense of the whole community of life:

> If you talk to animals they will talk with you
> and you will know each other.
> If you do not talk to them you will not know them
> And what you do not know you will fear.
> What one fears one destroys.

Just as the early plants, fungi family and insects are flourishing on planet Earth and the oceans teeming with life, the first great extinction on record occurs. This is due to climate change. A great ice age chilled the Earth, exterminating more than half of all species. The recovery period was long and arduous spanning about 25 million years. Bacteria and protists survived the ordeal and formed the food chain for surviving and emerging larger species. We know that even though life depends almost totally on the self-giving of the Sun, there are bacteria existing deep within the oceans surrounding volcanic vents, caves and ocean bed hot springs. These alone flourish without the life-giving energy of the Sun as they feed on raw material of chemicals dissolved in water.

### Amphibians Skip Ashore

The mudskipper fish symbolises this new phase in land exploration. Here is a creature leading a double lifestyle as it were – at sea and on land, namely 'amphibious'. We see them today, these four-footed vertebrates, in muddy estuaries and mangrove swamps or relaxing on the mud beyond the river's edge. They come to feed on insects and other invertebrates nestling in the oozy mud and scamper back to the safety of the water when disturbed.

Amphibians interact and co-evolved with the early plants and fungi. Today salamanders, newts and frogs embody most closely the appearance of the early ones. The amphibians invented the extendable tongue, which is useful in search of prey. The first amphibians emerged about 370 million years ago. They have small lungs and breathe partly through their skin. This can happen only if the skin is damp, hence their tendency to live near water. One of the great challenges facing them was to survive and breed in areas with little or no rain or water tracts. Evolutionary creativity came to the rescue once more in the form of reptiles to create a watertight skin and a watertight egg.

Reptiles evolved from the amphibians and dominated the Earth for over 200 million years. They were the first beings to create eggs with a protective covering. This enabled them to deposit them inland far from predators and with their ever-evolving watertight skin they were able to roam far and wide. Wandering in forest and desert they eventually crowded out the amphibians. There are about six thousand different kinds of reptile: crocodiles, alligators, turtles, tortoises, lizards, dinosaurs and snakes (these latter have no legs). The next breakthrough invention of the land animal was to develop a technique of maintaining body warmth, particularly in the face of a cold outer surface (endothermy). This capability of 'warm-blooded reptiles' was a highly significant step in the history of life. At this time primitive clubmoss forests and seed ferns gave birth to conifer trees and plants. They live in a moss around the root where they find protection and in turn provide nourishment for the trees. The process of mutual nourishment initiated by the alchemy of photosynthesis in the distant past continues to weave through the entire community of life.

## Dinosaurs

Dinosaurs, the name means 'terrible lizards', dominated the land for almost 160 million years from about 220 million years ago. They were one of the most successful species ever to have inhabited planet Earth. Among their contemporaries were the crocodiles. Dinosaurs became extinct about 65 million years ago. Paleontologists (people who study fossil remains) are divided as to why and how they disappeared after such a long reign as Earth's dominant species. It may have been as a result of volcanic activity causing temperature change or, as is the more popular belief, that a massive asteroid collided with planet Earth sending shock waves that killed vegetation thus causing starvation. In Mexico, at Chicxulub, there stands a huge crater where a meteor hit the Earth 65 million years ago and may have terminated the dinosaur mastery of the planet. Could it have been a more gradual process? No one knows for certain. It is known that dinosaurs are the most intriguing and spectacular of all extinct animals. The tragedy, whatever it was, was so powerful that all communities of insects, flowers and fungi, reptiles, mammals and emerging birds, as well as the luxuriant forests were destroyed beyond recognition.

Mammals evolved from the reptiles some two hundred and twenty million years ago. However, the mammals were only able to flourish after the dinosaurs were eliminated about 65 million years ago. Living as it were in the shadow of the giant dinosaurs, mammals were unable to diversify. Ecological niches left by giant reptiles were now available for other animals. At this time the Earth's plates were shifting, cracking apart and moving away from each other. The Atlantic Ocean was shaped, separating the Eurasian and American continents, heralding the break up of Pangaea, the Earth's super continent.

## On a Wing and a Song

For millions of years insects were enjoying the freedom of the skies; soon they were to have company. About 150 million years ago the first birds evolved from small dinosaurs and Earth resounded with birdsong. They were the first feathered creatures. Birds live everywhere on planet Earth, from the wandering albatross to the swimming penguin, the soaring golden eagle to the fast-running, flightless emu. The ostrich, taller than the human, is the largest bird while the bee-hummingbird, the robin and song thrush are small enough to fit in the palm of one's hand. Birds are the only feathered species, which enables them to keep warm as well as assisting in flying. I am amazed when I take a moment to salute the migratory birds on their long journeys to warmer zones. How do they know where to go, store enough sustenance for the flight and fly in formation with changing front leaders? Do they, as suggested in the film *Winged Migration*, look out for landmarks on the way? It is as intriguing as the spawning habits of salmon, their kin in the waters, travelling dangerously upstream, back home to birth their young.

### Seeds of Life

About 120 million years ago, after almost 4.5 billion years of evolutionary development, planet Earth birthed flowering plants. This was an awesome moment. These flowering plants concentrate their life energy in seed thereby making protein available for mammals. This emergence bathes the Earth's ecosystems in colour and fragrance in the form of flowers and fruit. They are called flowering plants because they reproduce by means of flowers. They belong to a group known as *angiosperms*, which include grasses, common flowers and broadleaved trees. The wind and animals join in the process of pollination and fertilisation. Insects are the primary animal pollinators, particularly bees and butterflies, who are attracted by the senses of smell and sight (colour). While they are in search of nectar, pollen grains stick to their bodies, some of which is left behind on the next flowers the insects visit. The wind carries pollen grains far and wide. Birds are active in the process of seed dispersal. They consume berries. The tougher seeds pass out intact through their droppings and sprout again.

## The Miracle of Mammals

When we think of animals we usually mean mammals. This is because we know them best since many of our domesticated animals are mammals – dogs, cats, horses and cattle. There is also the fact of their large brain and intelligence. Mammals are of two types: marsupials and placental. The former give birth to very undeveloped offspring, which they nurture in pouches outside their bodies, for example, the kangaroo, wombat, koala and opossum. The latter develop the embryo fully within the body of the mother and nourish their offspring from their own body substance, for example, the weasel, deer, hare, tiger, bat, hippopotamus, human. Marsupials are found mainly in New Guinea, Australia and the Americas. Most mammals are placental, inhabiting every part of the world: forests, seas, deserts, the Arctic regions and temperate zones. Some are plant-eating, called herbivores, some flesh-eating, carnivores, mainly predators and parasites, and some are both, forming the food web in the community of life.

Mammals are a very diverse group: whales live in the water, bats fly, monkeys climb, horses gallop and dogs run. They share certain characteristics: warm-blooded, bony, with lungs, some fur/hair on their bodies and all feed their offspring on milk. Among mammals, the brain expansion of one particular group has enabled them to occupy unique ecological niches in the Earth's ecosystems. These are the primates, including bush babies, lemurs, monkeys, apes and humans – emerging some 70 million years ago:

> Their special adaptations relate to agility in trees and the complex social interactions of forest life;

exceptional brain-power, keen eyesight with stereoscopic vision, and extended parental care.[6]

The stage is now set for the emergence of the early hominids culminating in *homo sapiens sapiens* between 2 and 7 million years ago.

## The Profundity of Life

Our extraordinary evolutionary story brings home to us the absolute mystery of life, the profundity of God and the divine creative genius over the past 13 billion years. Central to our cosmic identity is the fact that every living being is related to every other living being, together we form the intricate web of life, the sacred community of the universe:

> Quantum theory forces us to see the universe not as a collection of physical objects, but rather as a complicated web of relations between the various parts of a unified whole.[7]

Our ancestral heritage reaches all the way back to the atoms spewed out in the original flaring forth. What a journey! We have been there from our bacterial ancestors, who created oxygen and invented every metabolic process known today, through the trials and breakthrough moments of species emergence and the violence and competitive aggression as well as cooperation and mutual support. Teilhard de Chardin (1881-1955) had a profound sense of the interconnectedness of life. He told the story of the universe in an integral manner, perhaps for the first time. In his book *The Phenomenon of Man*, he emphasised the fact that the galactic, earth, life and human stories are one story. The human story is integral to the earth story. For Teilhard, matter possessed a psychic-spiritual as well as a physical dimension, all of life was in the original fireball and has been evolving ever since:

> To live the cosmic life is to live dominated by the consciousness that one is an atom in the body of the mystical and cosmic Christ.[8]

## The Earth is Alive

The integral story of the universe is challenging us to make the shift from seeing ourselves as beings on the Earth to knowing that we are beings of the Earth, we are the Earth, the Universe, reflecting on its 13 billion years of unbroken evolutionary magnificence. We now understand that Earth is not, as most of us have thought for so long, a planet merely sustaining life. It is a living planet. Earth is alive. Scientists tell us that earth during the 4.5 billion years of its history has maintained its average body temperature even though the Sun's temperature has increased significantly. The chemical composition of its atmosphere and the salinity of the oceans have also been maintained in a manner that is only possible for a living system. This idea of a living planet is known as the 'Gaia Hypothesis', the active biological control of the environment to suit itself rather than the earth's atmosphere creating conditions for life. James Lovelock supported by Lynn Margulis and influenced by the experience and information of the early astronauts proposed the Gaia Hypothesis in the early 1970s. Beholding the Earth from space was for many of these early lunar pioneers from the late 1960s a mystical and deeply moving experience:

From the Moon, Earth is so small and so fragile, and such a precious little spot in the Universe, that you can block it out with your thumb. Then you realize that on that spot, that little blue and white thing, is everything that means anything to you – all of history and music and poetry and art and death and birth and love, tears, joy, games, all of it right there on that little spot that you can cover with your thumb. And you realize from that perspective that you've changed forever... (Rusty Schweickart, astronaut, USA).

Earth, the garden planet and our home, is a living organism. Ours is the privilege of celebrating the profusion and magnificence of the whole community of the universe, the profundity of existence, filled with awe and wonder at the mystery of God, whatever we perceive the divine to be:

The heavens are telling the glory of God; and the firmament proclaims his handiwork. Day to day pours forth speech, and night declares knowledge. There is no speech, nor are there words; their voice is not heard; yet their voice goes out through all the earth, and their words to the end of the world. (Psalm 19: 1-4).

## Notes

1. *A Walk through Time* by S. Liebes, E. Sahtouris and B. Swimme, 191, (John Wiley & Sons, Inc. New York, 1998).
2. As quoted in *Original Blessings* by Matthew Fox, 132, (Bear & Company Santa Fe, New Mexico).
3. Anthony De Mello *The Song of the Bird*, 99, (Image Books, Doubleday New York, London 1984).

4. As quoted in *Original Blessings*, 88.
5. *Life on Earth* by David Attenborough, 106, (Fontana, British Broadcasting, Corporation 1979).
6. *Atlas of Evolution* by Cassells Part V, 288, (Cassell & Co. London, 2001).
7. *The Tao of Physics* by Fritzjof Capra, 150, (Shambhala, Boulder Co., 1991).
8. *Writings in Time of War* by Teilhard de Chardin, 70, (Collins, 1968).

# OUT OF THE TREES

## The Universe Shivers With Wonder in the Depths of The Human
### Brian Swimme

It was coming towards the end of the spring season. The hedgerows were showing off their new foliage as I rambled down a country lane. The primroses were especially eye-catching in their shimmering delicacy. I stopped to look at a couple of clusters poised on the extending roots of a sycamore tree; they were like unruly toes on its bony feet. Their gentle movement in the soft breeze created a sense of liveliness, as if the great earthy feet were limbering up for take-off. I was reminded of the first time I saw a human skeleton, adult size, in a museum – the frame was like a great trunk with extending branches while the bones radiated like roots into the soil. At that moment I knew in my bones that we share the same sap, the same life-blood that flows though all of creation.

There is a Pacific Island proverb: 'To know where we are going, first we have to know who we are and where we came from.' Where precisely did the first human beings live on planet Earth? What did they look like? What sort of environment greeted their emergence? When did they come down from the trees? Some time between 2.6 and 7 million years ago the fiery gaseous matter of the original flaring forth

– shifting and changing over almost 14 billion years and creating the wonderful array of beings in the community of life – was in labour birthing the human being. The human was born into the order of the primates, which includes the lemurs, tarsiers, monkeys and apes. Originally there was only a single group of primates (c. 65 – 55 million years ago), but this became more expansive and diversified so that forty thousand years ago there were large numbers of primates roaming the European and Asian continents.

A further development occurred in Africa with the emergence of a fox-sized primate in the Upper Nile region around 30 million years ago. This particular primate, the first to appear on the African continent, manifested an anatomy and teeth, which would eventually characterise developed apes. It was on an island in Lake Victoria in east-central Africa, that an ape with a brain capacity of over 150 cubic centimetres first appeared. Notably, the tail was no longer part of the anatomy. Later expansion of the primates in Africa included the gibbon, orang-utan, gorilla and chimpanzee leading to the hominids (upright, two-footed primal mammal). Steve Bloom, the South African born, internationally-renowned special-effects photographer, expresses our close kinship when he exclaims: 'Gaze into the eyes of a gorilla and you will be changed forever.' The gorilla is about 98 per cent similar in DNA to the human, the chimpanzee is even closer, sharing some 98.4 per cent DNA. Jane Goodall, UK wildlife activist, pioneered a study of wild chimpanzees in Tanzania's Gombe National Park in 1960. Her findings are enlightening:

> We had no idea how like us they really are: the close lifelong friendships between family members; the acts

of altruism; the communication gestures such as kissing, embracing, holding hands; the tool-using and tool-making skills. And they have a culture too: a newly acquired behaviour may be passed to successive generations through observation, imitation and practice. It humbles us, this knowledge – it blurs the line once thought so sharp, dividing humans from the rest of the animal kingdom.[1]

## Hominid to Human: A Balancing Act

When exactly did the first human emerge? This is the subject of intensive ongoing research. The African continent is the undisputed home of the human being, but where in this vast continent did we first come down from the trees and walk upright? Until recently, scientists and palaeontologists (who study fossil remains of ancient beings), believed that the first hominid lived in southern Ethiopia some four million years ago. This young female, known as 'Lucy', possessed a brain capacity of between four and five hundred cubic centimetres. This was slightly greater than that of the chimpanzee. She represents the *Australopithecus afarensis* species. Genetic research carried out by Hawaiian geneticist Rebecca Cann and colleagues almost twenty years ago confirms this view. They published the first 'mitochondrial DNA' (mtDNA) tree showing the long line of ancestry back to a single African female ancestor. Two very important elements in DNA research are the 'Y chromosome' (which passes down the male line from our fathers) and the 'mitochondrial DNA', or mtDNA, (which passes down the female line from our mothers). Using technology that sequences our DNA, genetic research is based on the fact that although most of our DNA gets spliced and reshuffled through fertilisation, there are two tiny elements that remain intact: the Y chromosome and the mtDNA, pass intact from generation to generation.

The discovery of a skull in Kenya by Kenyan researchers on a National Geographic Society expedition in 1998-99 has, however, sparked fresh ponderings about human ancestry. This skull, which scientists named *kenyanthropus platyops*, is 3.5 million years old, thus coming from roughly the same time period as 'Lucy' from Ethiopia. A more recent report in the journal *Nature*, July 2001, reveals a newfound ancestor, a chimp-sized creature living in the Ethiopian forests between 5.2 million and 5.8 million years ago. An Ethiopian graduate student, Yohannes Haile-Selassie, enrolled in a US university, unearthed the remains of what appears to be the most ancient ancestor ever to be discovered. The intriguing thing about this discovery is that it locates human emergence very close to the time when chimpanzees and humans first embarked on their separate evolutionary journeys.[2]

A further development occurred in 2001 with the discovery by French researchers of *orrorin tugenensis*, 'Original Man' from Tugen Hills, Kenya. Cranial and post-cranial fragments show a direct link to bipedalism 6 million years ago. The latest find, a skull unearthed in 2002 in the Chad region of Africa by French archaeologists, indicates that human ancestry could be as old as seven million years. Using the image of our family tree, are we talking about more than one trunk, perhaps even more than a single tree? Darwin proposed the image of a coral, noting that the base is long gone, while the tips alone remain. Of the discoveries to date: which one is ancestral to the earliest species of *homo* (the latin word for 'man'), the precursor of modern humans? Alternatively, might *homo* have evolved separately within the community of life?

*Homo genus*

Whatever the origin we do know that the main division is centred between the rather small-brained *australopithecines* and the larger-brained, fully two-footed *homo*. Are there more than one species of *homo*? Where do the Neanderthals (named after the Neander Valley, Germany) fit in the emergence of modern humans? Many scientists regard the several generally recognised species of *homo* 'as merely geographical variants of the normal anatomical variations that are usually encountered in any population'.[3] The earliest expression of the *homo* genus emerged about 2.5 million years ago in the Turkana region of northwest Kenya. Designated *homo habilis* or 'handy man', this early human form was distinguished by the ability to make and use tools. While earlier hominids manifested a slight increase in brain size and were able to stand upright and use tools on occasion, there is no evidence to suggest that theirs was a reasoned response to life and their environment.

What can we glean from fossil remains discovered by anthropologist Louis Leakey about *homo habilis*? We learn little in terms of the thought patterns and cultural life. *Homo habilis* had a more rounded skull and brain size of some seven hundred cubic centimetres, smaller teeth and overall more refined features than their predecessors. *Homo habilis* stood firmly on two legs and weighed around forty kilograms. The ability to walk must have developed over a long period of time. How many tumbles, bruises, even giggles characterised the learning process? Although our earliest ancestors would have continued to live in the trees as well as in the open savannah, it must have seemed strange at first to be looking up from the vantage point of *terra firma*. What about the sense of wonder and awe gazing into the open sky away from foliage and forest canopies? What did the texture of earth feel

like compared to the trees? What of the feelings of
exhilaration and freedom, of playfulness or of fear and
vulnerability? One wonders whether the birds missed their
branch companions. Did the trees experience a sense of loss
and loneliness, or perhaps relief? Does the land experience
similar feelings about us today? We must at least ask these
questions.

This was indeed a sacred moment. The land of soil,
grass, waterways and mountains opened its expansive arms
to greet the new arrivals. Who could have imagined what
was to unfold over the coming millennia? The universe
shuddered as through the human it fashioned possibilities
hitherto unimagined, dreams wild beyond contemplation,
beauty mirroring the creation of long ago stars and galaxies
and passions bewildering in their intensity and
contradictions. The human is the being in whom the Earth
becomes conscious of itself in reflective self-awareness.
Teilhard de Chardin expressed this privilege thus: 'The
human person is the sum total of unbroken evolution now
thinking about itself.' The fruits of human presence
nurtured by the natural beauty and fluorescence of Earth:
imagination, thoughts, dreams; music, dance, poetry, art,
literature, sport, farming, technology, sacred ceremonies
and faith commitments span the eons of eternity like jewels
in Indra's net,[4] a shining testimony to 'being charged with
the grandeur of God'. What a privilege. What a
responsibility.

We have our collective shadow-side as a species among
species. We can mess things up, lose the sense of who we are,
become paranoid, greedy, consumerist, conquering, paralysed.
There is the need for constant vigilance, balance, facing reality
and acknowledging our place. The welcoming land that we first

stepped on with hesitancy and respect is now sadly taken largely for granted by many of us. All too soon the earth was to experience the power of human technology, initially this was relatively benign (in the form of hand-axes, choppers, flint hollow scrapers and knives), but later it became more aggressive. Technology in itself is good and does much to enhance the quality of life. How it is used, by whom, for what purpose and at what cost to the community of all life, these are the critical issues.

It is sobering to consider that our lineage began in an ocean home, then an arboreal nest; today the water, the forests and land are all at risk from human ignorance and greed. It is as if we have forgotten where we came from and who is nurturing us. It is time to wake up, to come down from our perches of viewing Earth as 'out there' separate from us and return the primal embrace of hospitality, of oneness, of home. We are not simply beings *on* planet Earth, but rather beings *of* the Earth. We are the Earth-conscious. How do we exercise this privilege and responsibility?

Generally speaking, other species tend to operate out of a give-and-take system of mutual nourishment, taking only what they need. We don't seem to be satisfied with some trees, we must fell entire forests, extract finite resources until depletion, create mountains of waste that could suffocate entire species, including ourselves. We continue to enlarge our 'ecological footprint' on planet Earth far in excess of its carrying capacity. The authors of *Our Ecological Footprint* are cautionary:

> The present ecological footprint of a typical North American represents three times his/her fair share of

the Earth's bounty. Indeed, if everyone on the Earth lived like the average Canadian or American we would need at least three such planets to live sustainably.[5]

We in the western world, in particular, have the audacity to claim ownership of Mother Earth, to patent rights over parts of the cosmic womb that birthed us and the entire community of life – water rights, land rights, seed rights, food rights, timber-logging rights, mineral and chemical rights. Most arrogantly of all, we claim superiority over all beings in the cosmic community and place human rights solely at the centre of all our systems – economics, politics, health, education, religion and so on – systems which are non-aligned with the whole earth system. Another way of saying this is that a mere few million years ago the human arrived on what is truly no man's land, that is, home to all people and every species. Over the centuries humans have endeavoured to make it the property of the few to the exclusion of the many – other people and life forms. The journey home is a long one. The challenge facing us is that of reconnecting with our deepest roots, the soul wisdom of the oneness of all life. I believe that understanding how we got here is central to this process. We will examine the human journey for some clues as to how we can proceed in a more mutually enhancing way as the whole community of life, the one sacred community of the universe.

### Hunter-Gatherer and Stone Crafter

I suppose it is fair to assume that if anyone were to say to you or me today that our parents were scavengers we would be outraged. Yet when we stop to consider our deepest ancestral roots we realise that, even though the term 'scavenge' was not coined before the seventeenth century, it aptly describes our early forebears as they roamed in search of food. Perhaps I would be even more outraged if someone were to deem me a scavenger. It may be nearer the bone than many of us care to admit even to ourselves. Consider the unequal distribution of wealth, of food and education, the ravishing of earth's bountifulness, the usurpation of rights and freedoms with regard to the whole community of life. One grimaces in dismay as the very fabric of life is systematically weakened before the scavenging of greedy developers and multinational corporations. Can we dismiss our scavenging traits? Even more, can those of us living a more consumerist life style acknowledge that we are thereby subjecting others – humans, birds and animals – to a more scavenging mode of living. And we have the audacity to complain when the economically disadvantaged ask for what is theirs or the fox turns up at the back door of our city apartment.

The Great Rift Valley of Kenya, specifically in the region of Olduvai, could be described as a massive tool-shed for our early ancestors. The variety and number of stone implements discovered point to the fact that they were most likely used in capturing and preparing animals for food. The evidence from the type of tools and clothing as well as from the teeth structure of these early humans shows that they were hunters as well as gatherers. The making of tools marked a decisive stage in the evolutionary development of the human, a growing sense of their own power over other life forms, animals as well as plants. This marked the beginning of the Stone Age. Working with stone required thought and imagination and besides the utility factor there emerged a growing aesthetic sense in terms of shape, proportion and variety. In these transition years significant foundations were being established:

> The sense of time and place was developing; imagination was receiving the impress of its most powerful images; the stock of primordial memories that would influence all future generations was being developed; an intimate rapport between the human and the natural world was being established, a rapport that was filled with both the terror and the attraction of the surrounding wilderness. The ever-recurring sequence of seasonal decline and renewal was making its impress on the human psyche as one of the most basic patterns that would later find expression in ritual celebration.[6]

*Homo Erectus*

The Turkana region of Africa is the most likely location for the emergence of *homo erectus* over 1.5 million years ago, the same region where many of their predecessors had lived. The fossil remains discovered at Koobi Fora in Kenya, dating to 1.7 million years ago, are among the earliest of *homo erectus* and confirm a significant increase in brain size. *Homo erectus*, or 'upright man', possessed a tall, long-legged physique and the ability to walk fully upright. The ability to use the legs is all-important in that it left the hands free for manipulation, which in turn led to greater creativity. It facilitated great prowess in adapting to a wide range of environments. This particular species of early human flourished throughout the continent of Africa and initiated the first grand migration of peoples out of Africa. *Homo erectus*, also known as 'Java man' and 'Sinanthropus' ('Chinese man') travelled extensively in Asia and Europe over the next million years, often living in caves.

## Fire on the Earth

Among the stone tools made and used by *homo erectus* were choppers, awls, chisels, scrapers and hand axes. Wood and bone were also used in tool making. Skins of animals were used in the erection of shelters and for clothing. There are quite extensive remains of ashes, charred clays and burnt bones signifying the use of fire. This is significant in that it manifests human control of a powerful natural force with almost unlimited possibilities, a unique symbolism recalled thousands of years later by Teilhard de Chardin, French palaeontologist and Jesuit priest:

> The day will come when after we have mastered the winds, the waves, the tides and gravity, we will harness for God the energies of love. Then for the second time in the history of the world, man will have discovered fire.[7]

Fire provided warmth, which was especially necessary as our ancestors moved further north into Eurasia, and was used in food preparation. In addition the hearth fire became a place of bonding, of communion, of security and of relaxation. Did our ancestors use what we understand as language today to share experiences or discuss hunting tactics? Fossil remains have so far been unable to yield this sort of information, but it is widely believed that the evolving human sounds were more complex, slower and less clumsy than the screams of modern apes. In addition, the emerging human had another medium of communication – gesture. It is a fact that human beings have more separate facial muscles than any other animal.[8] The flexibility of lips, cheeks, eyebrows and forehead is pertinent here. Facial expression transmits meaning. It can convey intentions: nod or shake of the head, as well as changing moods: delight, anger, fear, amusement. The role played by gestures in communication is evident today among some smaller, more geographically remote tribes, for example, Biami, in New Guinea, and some Aborigines.

## The Allure of Beauty: Mythological stirrings

The internationally renowned American anthropologist, Joseph Campbell, speaking of *homo erectus* and the shaping of our mythic tradition, points out that there are two kinds of human: the animal human being who is practical (tool maker, hunter-gatherer) and the human-human being, who 'is susceptible to the allure of beauty'. He refers to tools found on the banks of the river Thames, their size (much larger than practical tools), indicating their use in a ritual context.[9] I find this image enlightening as we try to unravel our ancestral heritage. Where do I fit in this view? Perhaps a more accurate question might be: to what extent am I susceptible to the allure of beauty, to the divine extravagance in the universe?

My father played the melodeon
Outside at our gate;
There were stars in the morning east
And they danced to his music.
Patrick Kavanagh[10]

*Homo Sapiens – Homo sapiens neanderthalensis*
A decisive new development occurred in north central and east Africa about two hundred thousand years ago: *homo sapiens* emerged, succeeding *habilis* and *erectus* and known as 'ape man', from which contemporary humans are descended.

A second great wave of migrations coincided with the emergence of *homo sapiens*; this brought the human far beyond the African-Eurasian world to the American continent and to Australia by forty thousand years ago. The development of the Neanderthals *(homo sapiens neanderthaensis)*, in the Neander Valley of Germany can be traced in Europe for 400,000 years. Where did they originate? Do they form a separate family tree? Why and how did they become extinct leaving not a trace? These questions are the subject of much debate. In fact for most of the twentieth century scientists viewed this early type of human with disdain: 'huge and ungainly, with a heavy and powerful body, a head whose robust skull – and jawbones – manifest the prevalence of purely animalistic, instinctive functions over mental processes.'[11] Neanderthals had certain specialised skull features: bony bulges above the eye sockets, flat cheekbones, a prominent nose, receding chin and very large teeth. They had a brain capacity of fifteen hundred cubic centimetres, which is slightly larger than that of the average modern human.

They appear to have lived in complex social groupings and were very resourceful in adapting to a variety of different habitats and harsh climates. They knew how to use fire, to make advanced tools from rocks and bones and to hunt large animals for food and clothing. Among the animals they hunted down were bison, deer, gazelle and goats, as well as birds and fish on occasion. Could these people speak? It is not known for certain, but the fact that they lived in complex groupings of small bands indicates that there was presumably some form of communication. One characteristic of the Neanderthals was their care for the dignity of their deceased. Their burials are clear evidence that they had developed fairly elaborate cultural rituals. The discovery of the Neanderthal burial site at Kebana in Israel, which is approximately 60,000 years old is representative of many such burials, which often included items to sustain the deceased in the afterlife and their journey back to life. This attention to their deceased has led to a revision of the earlier expressed view that Neanderthals were primitive, fearsome and often brutal.

## Mythological rumblings

*Homo sapiens*, Wise Man/Woman gives us more insight into the early signs of mythological thinking particularly through their small cave-bear chapels and burial rituals. The bear cult was significant at this time in human emergence. It is still practised by the Ainu, the ethnic group making up the indigenous population of the island of Hokkaido in northern Japan. An animal was seen as a willing sacrifice, highly revered by these people. There is evidence of this cult from discoveries high in the Alps in Switzerland of small stone-ringed cave-bear chapels where cave-bear skulls were worshipped. Among the Ainu today the cave bear is sacred, central to their ceremonies. The elements, all growing and living things are accorded great respect and thanked for the giving of their substance for nourishment:

> Trees, our old people said, hold water which comes forth from the earth when it is needed. Trees on mountains, too, are the homes of our bear and deer. We were taught to respect our rivers and not to pollute them. They were the home of our fish.[12]

The ceremonial practice of the Neanderthals about the Middle Palaeolithic (Stone Age) period manifests the beginnings of a religious mode of consciousness. They were beginning to associate identity, meaning and belief with quite elaborate burial rituals. The intricate arrangement of stones at the burial site is a mythic, ritual response to the mystery of life hidden in the rhythms and melodies of the universe.

For our early forebears there must have been a moment of decision, of interpretation, as the rhythm of birthing and passing away became obvious. Before the Neanderthals there is no evidence of attention to deceased members, we can only presume that their bodies were cast aside as occurs among other primates. There was the sequence of the seasons, the dying of winter and the renewal of spring, sequences that were influential in evolving human consciousness and vulnerability. These profound manifestations of the cosmological order evoked wonder, awe, fear and reverence and invited participation:

> The universe was a dramatic reality, filled with powers and voices, constituting the Great Conversation that humans participated in through daily and seasonal rituals as well as through rituals associated with birth, maturity, and death.[13]

The unearthing of ritual burial sites from this time in Northern Iran and Iraq signify close connections with Mother Earth. Remains show the foetal position in death among animals and humans indicating a return to the womb, the cosmic nurturer of life and peaceful repose in death. The people needed a rapport with the spirits of the phenomenal world, a power that was regarded as all-pervasive and controlling the origin and destiny of all beings. A burial site discovered in Lebanon reveals a sacrificial aspect to these symbolic rituals. A slaughtered deer placed with the deceased within a pattern of painted stones, signifies a consciousness of the mystery of death and the longing for the return of the deceased whether human or animal. Death remains a mystery; how often have we heard it said in face of the passing of a loved one 'no body returns to tell us what is beyond'.

*Homo sapiens sapiens*

Around 30,000 to 35,000 years ago all trace of the Neanderthals vanished. What could have caused the demise of such a powerful race after some 150,000 years? This remains a mystery. Could it have been through natural causes? We know from research in human population growth patterns that within the relatively short space of a millennium an entire population can be wiped out with a mere one to two per cent rise in death rate. Perhaps it was a combination of natural causes combined with the absorption of surviving members into the modern *homo sapiens* peoples recently arrived on the scene. Where did *homo sapiens sapiens*, or modern human, originate? The location is most likely Africa with migrations reaching Europe possibly from the Middle East. In Europe these people became known as the Cro-Magnon after the discovery in 1868 of a cave along the banks of the river Vezere in France. This cave housed the grave of three men, one woman and one child in the area called Cro-Magnon. Research would indicate that the Neanderthals and Cro-Magnon co-existed for approximately ten thousand years in the area of modern Israel and for some five thousand years in France. Did competition develop between them, the struggle for supremacy or survival in the harsh, icy conditions? We can only surmise.

## Last Advance of the Ice Ages

This Ice Age in the Northern Hemisphere, which began around 75,000 years ago, covered much of Europe and North America during the emergence of the modern human or Cro-Magnon. The Arctic weather conditions tested their ingenuity as the biosystems of the planet were in a state of change. Many plant and animals species retreated south to survive until the ice diminished with the recession, which began around 18,000 years ago and continues today. People used wood, bone, antlers and hide to build more durable shelters from the glacial chill and to create new and sharper tools. Fire was important for heat, light, cooking and security. In addition, lamps were used extensively with animal fat as fuel. Spear throwers, harpoons and bows and arrows were used extensively in hunting larger game. This was undoubtedly a factor in the eventual disappearance of some of the mega-forms of life like the mammoth and woolly mastodon. Other causes included climate and, in the light of current research, diseases, spread possibly by dogs and other domesticated animals that came in touch with these larger animals. The harsh climactic conditions were compounded by new and widespread volcanic activity throughout planet Earth.

Throughout the Ice Age, Ireland was part of mainland Europe. At various stages much of the country was covered by an ice-cap, similar to the Arctic today. Over the thousands of years the cold and warm conditions see-sawed as the ice advanced and retreated over the country. During the last cold stage, the midlands and northern parts were completely ice-covered for short periods while the southern parts of Munster were free of the pressure of ice. Therefore the woolly mammoth, reindeer, the giant Irish deer and the arctic fox were free to roam in the grassy landscape. Ireland and Britain were separated from mainland Europe early in the postglacial period. The two islands were connected by land bridges for about 1500 years before Ireland became a separate island some time between 10,000 and 5,700 BCE. A wide variety of plants and animals crossed the land bridges, for example, pine, elm, birch, red deer, wild boar, pine-martens, red squirrels, foxes, stoats, wolves, eagles and other birds of prey. When Ireland became an island, the days of easy migration were over. Henceforth, any animal who couldn't swim or fly could only make the journey by means of human intervention. Long after the connection between Ireland and England was severed due to climate change (rapid rise in post-glacial sea level), England was still a peninsula of Europe. Thus the northward migration of plants and animals into lands abandoned by the ice continued to colonise England for some time after the flow to Ireland had been cut off. As a result, England developed a much greater variety of plants and animals; Ireland's natural environmental record being approximately thirty per cent less.

### Awakening the Artist

What is it that distinguishes the human from all other animals? Is it making and using tools? Not any more since we realise that chimpanzees also use them. And, as David Attenborough reminds us, finches in the Galapagos Islands, cut and shape long thorns to use as pins to extract grubs from holes in wood. Perhaps it is in language? Even this is not certain now in light of the communications used by whales, dolphins and chimpanzees. However, as far as we know we are the only creatures to have painted pictures representing various aspects of the universe, particularly animals and birds. The Cro-Magnon people manifested an artistic skill and ingenuity of invention hitherto unknown among the long line of our human lineage.

Researchers have discovered hundreds of caves with people's engravings and wall paintings, the majority in France and Spain. There is also evidence of a variety of artistic traditions including the ochre-decorated rock shelters (Kisesse, East Africa), the rock art in areas of South Asia and the world's oldest rock engravings in Australia dating from 45,000 years ago. The unearthing of spectacular art galleries deep underground has stunned the world. In 1940 an amazing gallery of cave paintings was discovered at Lascaux in central France. These paintings of exceptional quality were seventeen thousand years old. In 1985, the professional diver Henri Cosquer, discovered a cave some thirty-five metres below sea level near Marseille in the south of France. These paintings, according to carbon-14 dating (analysis of charcoal used), are 28,000 years old. Finally, with the revelation of the exact dating of Chauvt's Cave discovered in 1995, the old notion that humankind needed many millennia to produce works of art is now obsolete. The sensation of this discovery in southern France puts earliest artistic genius at more than 33,000 years ago. What rich heritage we possess, why can't we all be artists?

## Earth: Great Mother Goddess

The spiritual journey of Earth's people began with the worship of a divine and powerful goddess. Early humans were conscious of their dependence on earth for all things, food, water, shelter and life itself. They were also aware that life emanated from the body of the female in various species so it was natural for them to see Mother Earth as the one who births, nourishes and sustains life. From about thirty-five thousand years ago a large number of small 'Venus' figures were created from a wide variety of materials such as ivory, wood, stone or tinted steatite (soapstone). In these there was special emphasis on the reproductive organs linked to fertility concerns and the Earth as the Great Mother provider.

Marija Gimbutas, Lithuanian-born, European archaeologist, in her book *The Language of the Goddess*, tells of how long before the advent of agriculture, female divinity was alive among the earliest peoples. They were reproducing the vulva, as well as seeds and sprouts in art. Some of these engravings have been found on rocks in caves in France – Abri Blanchard, La Ferraise and in the vicinity of Dordogne in southern France – as early as thirty thousand years ago. The stone figure of the Venus of Willendorf c. 20,000 BCE and the mammoth ivory carved pregnant female figure from Lespugne, France c. 25,000 BCE are other notable examples. The cosmic womb of the Goddess is the source of the waters of life, of birth and nurturance. The universe was seen as the living body of the Goddess Mother Creator with all living things within it partaking of her divinity.[14] The Irish expression of the fertility goddess is the 'Síle na gig'.

The goddess is the goddess of Nature. The unity of all life, the oneness of all created reality is at the heart of goddess worship. The goddess culture remained central in the lives of our ancestors around the world until about 1500 BCE when a combination of volcanoes, earthquakes and armed conflict buried it beneath the rubble of some of the great civilisations particularly in Malta, Crete and the Mediterranean region. The spirituality of the great goddess, of *Gaia*, Mother Earth, is dancing into life inviting us back to our roots, to re-connect as the human and natural world and find our place 'in the family of things'[15].

### Coded Wisdom

Why did our ancestors paint? Was it out of a sense of communion with their subjects? Was it for relaxation, to enjoy art for art's sake? Perhaps the designs were part of a religious ritual acknowledging the providence of the great goddess and influence of the spirit world in hunting expeditions, herd fertility and continuity. At any rate, for the emerging human with hands free, and directed by the human mode of consciousness, there were endless possibilities. As with every species, the human has to constantly adapt to changing circumstances, creating life-giving structures and meaning and establishing patterns hitherto unknown: 'Every species is in the process of creating and re-creating, both beneficially and detrimentally, its own conditions of existence, its own environment.'[16]

With artistic abilities there developed a whole new capacity for the understanding and use of spoken language. For the human acculturation was part of the developmental process. All other than human life forms are guided and directed primarily through their genetic coding, the human is genetically coded towards transgenetic cultural coding specifically invented by human communities in their particular environments. This can render one's approach to life, to attitudes, values and decision-making more complex. Do I evoke the wisdom of my genetic coding as well as my cultural coding in determining how to live with integrity in the whole community of life? I'm reminded of The Zen painter and poet, Kazuaki Tanahashi:

In thoughts today
my sleeves are wet
for the memory of dew
Travels into the mountains
of olden days.[17]

## One Day I Will Be An Ancestor

The Stone Age period when human beings lived by hunting, gathering and primitive stonecraft came to an end in Europe around eleven thousand years ago. The magnificent achievements of the Cro-Magnon were suddenly terminated. What was their legacy? Human beings, numbering over a million and occupying the various continents, were able to live with minimal intrusion into the life and functioning of planet Earth. They had created technologies for survival, while respecting the rights of other species. The cave sanctuaries, figurines, burial and other rites seem to indicate a belief in the intrinsic connectedness of all life – plant, animal, human – as emanating from the same source, the great goddess, the giver and nurturer of all life. Their artistic genius, belief in communion with the invisible and their sacred rituals reflected their wonder and awe, how they grappled with the mystery of life.

The Cro-Magnon lived in tune with the rhythms and melodies of the universe, conscious of the inner connectedness of all life. For these our early ancestors, life in all its manifestations was sacred, a mystery. Death was mysterious also, the deceased, whether human or animal, would come to life again, hence the care and ceremony of burial. They possessed a profound sense of our relatedness to the natural environment. Together we are integrally involved in the great mysteries of life and death, therefore, life, in all its forms, must be treated with reverence and respect. Like my Cro-Magnon forebears, I too will one day be an ancestor. What legacy would I like to bequeath to the community of the universe? What wisdom, what quality of life do I wish to pass on to the young of all species? My response will determine my attitudes, values, priorities, choices and decisions.

## Notes

1. *In Praise of Primates*, Steve Bloom, with a foreword by Dr Jane Goodall, 9 (Pubkönemann Verlagsgesellschaft MBH, Köln, Germany, 1999).
2. As reported in *Time*, July 23, 2001 'One Giant Step forward for Mankind'.
3. *Cassell's Atlas of Evolution* 318-9 (Andromeda Oxford Limited, 2001).
4. Indra is one of the chief deities in Indian mythology; he is reputed to be red and gold in colour and carrying a thunderbolt. When he struck the demon Bali with his thunderbolt, the slain demon's body gave rise to the seeds of various kinds of precious stones – diamonds, sapphires, rubies, emeralds, crystal, coral and pearls.
5. *Our Ecological Footprint*, Mathis Wackernagel and William E. Rees 13, (New Society Publishers British Columbia and CT, 1996).
6. *The Universe Story* 147-8 eds., Brian Swimme & Thomas Berry (HarperSanFrancisco, 1994).
7. Teilhard de Chardin *The Evolution of Chastity* quoted in 'Rediscovering Fire' by Ursula King 12 (Earthlight, Fall, 2000, Oakland, CA).

8. See *Life on Earth* by David Attenborough 'The Compulsive Communicators' for further information on the modes of communication of animals and early humans (Fontana, 1979).
9. *Mythos: The Shaping of our Mythic Tradition* Part 111 'On Being Human' (Joseph Campbell Foundation, USA, 1996).
10. 'A Christmas Childhood' 144 *Patrick Kavanagh: The Complete Poems* (The Goldsmith Press Co. Kildare, Ireland, 1984, 1987, 1988).
11. Marcellin Boule, Natural History Museum, Paris as quoted in *Last Mysteries of the World*, 16 (Reader's Digest (Australia) Pty Limited, 2000).
12. 'The Ainu of Japan' 126 in *The Way of the Earth* by T.C. Mc Luhan A Touchstone Book (Simon & Schuster New York, London Toronto, Sydney, Tokyo, Singapore, 1994).
13. *The Universe Story* eds., Brian Swimme & Thomas Berry 153 (HarperSanFrancisco, 1992).
14. *The Language of the Goddess*, Marija Gimbutas pgs 99ff. (HarperSanFrancisco, 1991).
15. *New And Selected Poems* by Mary Oliver 'Wild Geese' 110 (Beacon Press, Boston 1992).
16. *Genes, Environment and Organisms* by R.C. Lewontin in *Hidden Histories of Science* ed. Robert Silvers, 136 (London, 1977).
17. *Enku: Sculptor of a Hundred Thousand Buddhas*, Kazuaki Tanahashi, 8, (Shambhala Publications, Boulder, CO, 1982).

# Out of the Countryside

*We will be known forever by the tracks we leave*
Dakota

The wisdom of indigenous people echoes through the millennia. It is appropriate to draw on some of this guidance as we follow the ancient path of our human ancestors. The Haudenausenee native people, in their basic call to consciousness, tell us:

> In the beginning we were told that the human beings who walk about the Earth have been provided with all of the things necessary for life. We were instructed to carry love for one another, and to show a great respect for all the beings of this Earth. We were shown that our well-being depends on the well-being of the vegetable life, and that we are close relatives of the four-legged beings.[1]

Our hunter-gatherer ancestors gradually moved from the wide, open spaces to cluster in the major river valleys from where they weaved the great civilisations and evolved the major world religions. Groups of people still roam the countryside, the nomadic traits of old are still alive today in some areas of the world. There are universal themes that operate among all peoples and cultures, which connect us and link us together across the millennia. From earliest times people have been inspired and nourished by stories. Life is a search for meaning, but even more it is 'the experience of being alive'.[2] How to live in this world will always be a learning experience. It is an adventure that starts from within, in our psyche and soul. We have seen how people have tried to grapple with the mysterious in life, the mystery of God, of the universe, of life and death. The reality is that we participate in time, the historical sequence of events, while identifying with eternity. We have an inner world, the spiritual, which remains constant and an outer world, the arena of the historical, which is constantly changing. The vitality of myth is the link between these two worlds.

Myths (from Greek 'muthos') are stories that bring together the natural and supernatural. They point to the invisible behind the visible and bridge the inner and outer worlds. Touching deep, vivifying sources and profound mysteries, myths are indicators of the spiritual potentialities of life as these are lived in the richness and complexity of the whole community of creation: 'O Lord, how manifold are your works! In wisdom you have made them all; the earth is full of your creatures' (Ps. 104:24). Myths are a manifestation, an evocation of the cosmic energies within us, the pulsing life of the gods, the heavens and the earth. Another way of expressing the vitality of myth is to acknowledge its influence in our lives, enabling us to see life as a dance, a poem, a weaving, an adventure. We are participating with the divine energy in it. How did our early ancestors allow the mystical life to unfold? How did they go about living in the whole new world opening up before them? Their responses are embodied in farming, weaving, art and pottery, in fabrics, in tool-making, technology and architecture, in song, poetry, dance and ritual, in the Neolithic villages, in classical civilisations and in religious traditions.

## To Roam Or Not To Roam

The ice sheets retreated. Our hunter-gatherer ancestors moved further north and colonised northern Britain, northern Germany and Scandinavia. Humans reached the Americas from Siberia. It was c.10,000 BCE, marking over 4 million years of hunter-gatherer ancestry. Perhaps it was time to stop roaming and settle down. I wonder who suggested this and how it evolved? What were the plans, the discussions, disagreements, human factors and environmental influences on the way to agreement? Since the beginning humans had lived in groups of twenty-five to forty, moving from place to place on a monthly basis in search of food and shelter; they knew no other way. Nature was not so much a habitat, but rather a companion, a participant in the drama of life. The nomadic existence of a hunter-gatherer had to be uncluttered, simple and spontaneous; the present was all-important and movement always imminent. For people consistently on the move there was little room for prized possessions or heavy baggage.

From about twenty thousand years ago humans had progressively engaged in establishing relationships with particular plants and animals. They were, however, reluctant to stop roaming, it was in their bones – and it is in ours! There was a freedom and excitement with being on the move, which seemed to outweigh the hardships and perils. The movement into village life was slow and protracted. Among the deciding factors were most likely the challenge of climate, the stress of population and limited natural resources. The emergence of farming, the cultivation of various plants and seeds, together with the domestication of animals literally transformed the face of the Earth.

The process of selecting and propagating useful traits in wild crops occurred independently in several areas throughout the inhabited world. Each region developed particular staple crops: millet and rice in China and Southeast Asia, wheat and barley in the Middle East, bananas in Indonesia, sugar cane in New Guinea, maize in the Americas and grapes and olives in Greece and Crete. The first animal to be domesticated was the dog, valued for its hunting abilities and protection skills. Sheep and goats, native to West and Central Asia, were domesticated for their milk, meat, hides and wool. Gazelles, buffalo, pigs, chickens, and cattle became part of the settled community and provided it with food and clothing. Cattle were domesticated all over Eurasia and eventually used to draw the plough in crop farming, which increased the yield significantly. This mechanism is still used in some areas today.

## Early Village Life
The world's earliest farmers decided to settle in an area aptly known as the Fertile Crescent, an arc of land stretching from the Persian Gulf to the eastern Mediterranean. During the late Palaeolithic centuries, a shrine to the Great-Goddess in the Jordan region had become a popular gathering place. Around 8,000 BCE, permanent dwelling clusters began to emerge in this area, which came to be known as Jericho – the first Neolithic village. Huts of sun-dried bricks provided homes for around three thousand inhabitants. Jericho became a model of village life replicated in the numerous villages that sprang into being in these centuries. Humans became more

and more attuned to the natural rhythms and systems of the Earth. Their lives reflected the manner of winter silence, fallow time, becoming the spring song of life and newness. Large-seeded grains were domesticated in Jericho and, aware of the reproductive power of plants, seeds were tended and saved for the following year. Horticulture was born. Animals too belonged to Mother Earth. They were gradually domesticated and cared for as protectors and sources of food, clothing and shelter.

## Çatal Hüyük – sophisticated Stone Age settlement
In the region of Anatolia, known today as Turkey, a settlement of major significance was established c. 7,000 BCE in Çatal Hüyük. In the 1960s, a team of British archaeologists, led by James Mellaart, travelled to Turkey to excavate a mysterious mound. Their discovery of the remains of a large community dwelling was to revolutionise archaeological thinking. They were about to unearth one of the most elaborate and fascinating settlements ever discovered in the Middle East, Çatal Hüyük, a site 'which gave archaeologists the first tantalizing glimpse of an early farming settlement whose people cultivated cereals, crafted religious figurines, and traded with distant communities'.[3]

The unearthing of many small, carved figurines from early settlements throughout the Fertile Crescent gives some idea of the religious beliefs of our early ancestors. Many people seem to have worshipped some form of mother goddess and sometimes a young god associate. Notable examples include: the goddess enthroned, giving birth to a human child, supported by animals of the wild (Çatal Hüyük), and mother goddesses from Syria, Iran and Iraq. Elaborate burials, shrines and art objects indicate that ritual was central to the everyday lives of the people. As well as venerating the goddess as creator and provider, these early inhabitants venerated their ancestors. The discovered wall paintings and plaster art, often with silhouettes etched on the plaster, give some sense of a common religion throughout the settled region at this time. Birth is a recurring theme. Bulls' heads are a recurrent motif, almost certainly representing the male element. The cycles of birth and death are evidenced in ritual objects found at Çatal Hüyük and surrounding region:

> The richness of the ritual imagery at Çatal Hüyük hints at a high level of religious consciousness. Its nameless deities are the prototypes of later Anatolian gods and goddesses associated with birds, leopards, bulls, and deer.[4]

## The Agricultural Revolution

The cultivation of land, the planting of seeds and the harvesting of crops, was to alter forever the body of planet Earth. The more abundant crop yields enabled growth in population and brought large numbers of people together into settled village communities. The hunter-gatherer way of life continued in tandem for many years as people gradually, albeit reluctantly, moved towards larger groupings. As sedentary life emerged around agriculture, animals were tended communally and food surpluses supported the population over the colder winter months. This enabled some members of the community to develop a variety of craft skills, to engage in long-distance trade and to experiment with technology. With the development of agriculture, the perception of the Great Mother, as the all-pervasive creative and nurturing principle of the universe, was consolidated. At this time women played a central role in the affairs of society, both in its functioning and governance. They were seen as the source of its continued existence, initiators and artists and the creators of the basic crafts. Pottery was a momentous invention, which facilitated the carrying and storing of food. Gold and copper metallurgy developed earliest in the Middle East and the Balkans c. 6,500 BCE. Experiments with technology led to the discovery of irrigation with the first irrigated agriculture at Choga Mami in Iraq c. 5,500 BCE.

The emergence of towns and cities was a whole new venture for our ancestors, a reinvention of the human: 'The human world and the wilderness were progressively differentiated from each other. Natural processes such as the random dispersion of seeds, the flowing of streams and rivers, and the freedom of animals were altered by human intrusion.'[5]

At the end of the fourth millennium BCE, a change with far-reaching consequences occurred. For whatever reasons there was a shift from female deity-worship, which had dominated life since its beginnings, to male deity-worship. With the rise of technologies came the rise of men to more dominant roles in society. This in turn created a context for the emergence of Priest-Kings, who became the medium of human-divine and divine-human relations. For example, the Pharaoh in Egypt embodied the deity itself; in Sumer the leader or ruler was the representative of both people and deity as they interrelated, while in China the ruler received the divine mandate directly, with the explicit commission to bring about the unity of society and the entire cosmological order. The centrality of the great mother deity remained in the Minoan civilisation on the island of Crete until its destruction by both natural causes and warring invaders around 1459 BCE. The time of this transition to warring, male images of the divine was the era of megalithic stone structures, for example, Stonehenge (England), Newgrange, Knowth, Dowth, Carrowmore (Ireland) and Carnac (France).

## The Water of Life

About 3,500 years ago, humans discovered and began to inhabit the fertile areas near great rivers. The earliest civilisations grew up in the agriculturally rich valleys and alluvial plains of the rivers Tigris and Euphrates, Nile, Yellow River and the Indus River. One of the first of these was in Mesopotamia (named by the ancient Greeks and meaning 'between the rivers' – in this case the Tigris and the Euphrates). In an area of southern Mesopotamia, the Sumer region (now Iraq), was the birthplace of the earliest of the classical civilisations. Excavations reveal details of an astonishingly advanced people. The Sumerians, who flourished on the lower Euphrates c. 3,500 BCE, were destined to influence the course of history in a profound way. It was from Sumer and later Babylon (southern Mesopotamia) that a more conscious integration of the human and cosmological processes became explicit. The Sumerians were the first to develop a system of writing by sketching tiny pictures on clay tablets. Later this form changed as pictures were shortened into signs as manifested in the cuneiform script, many examples of which survive today. Mathematics began taking shape at this time – our three hundred and sixty degree circle and sixty-minute hour evolved here. The early study of astronomy and the signs of the zodiac with its particular symbolisations emerged in Mesopotamia.

## The Living Soil

The key to Sumer's richness was the soil. Situated between the two long rivers was a fertile area in the midst of a vast desert, the rich alluvial silt was the primary source of the area's wealth. The ability to grow crops proved advantageous, but irregular flooding remained a hazard. However, when people began to harness the water with dykes, reservoirs and canals the local economy was transformed. This was further enhanced with such vital advancements as the ox-drawn plough for tilling and the milking of animals to provide sustenance. The potter's wheel was invented about 3,400 BCE and this was subsequently adapted for transport thereby trebling the amount of goods carried at one time. Besides the increase in yield, these new inventions freed some people to become full-time craftspeople, traders and religious leaders. They constructed terraced ziggurats as sacred mountains and meeting places with the gods and goddesses. The Sumerians traded their agricultural produce, manufactured goods, woven garments and cloth for timber and metals. They learned how to make bronze, a yellowish-brown alloy of copper and tin. The period between 3,000-1,000 BCE is known as the Bronze Age after the widespread use of bronze. Gradually a number of city-states began to form in the Sumer region: Ur, Uruk, Nippur, Eridu. Unlike Egypt and its centralised form of government by a Pharaoh, who was seen as divine and possessing supreme power, Sumer consisted of dispersed city-states each with its own independent rule. This political structure was later developed by the Athenians in the Greek world and continued into the future. The Sumerians created legal codes; these formed the basis for later expansion in the period of Roman supremacy.

## From Tools to Weapons

The greatest city of ancient Mesopotamia was Babylon on the banks of the Euphrates River. Here King Hammurabi (1728-1686 BCE) built a vast and powerful empire, which lasted for over one thousand years. The established set of laws and code of conduct were known as the *Code of Hammurab*. As cities grew in size, and population and food production created surpluses, another major shift in human relationships was being created. With the abundance came warfare, a phenomenon that was to become chronic over the millennia. Our ancestors created tools for living; these were now being used as weapons for killing. One wonders what we have inherited, we too create tools for living through our technologies, but many of these are subtly becoming weapons. When does a vehicle for transport cease to be life-enhancing and become lethal on land, sea or sky? Even the humble kitchen knife becomes degraded in weaponry. The need to protect property eventuated in kingship, which in turn created the class system; hierarchies among peoples. The king was the locus of supreme power and authority with his army to defend and conquer. Kingship also facilitated the experience of individuality for the first time.

From these early stirrings of warfare we glimpse the consolidation of armed conflict as the means to so-called progress. The Babylonians under Nebuchadnessar II captured Jerusalem by force in 598 BCE and forced the Jewish people to live in Babylon: 'By the rivers of Babylon – there we sat down and we wept when we remembered Zion' (Psalm 137:1). The Psalmist's cry echoes down through the ages as people and land become more and more expendable. The radical shift from the Earth as partner has had, and continues to have dire consequences. After Babylon it was the turn of Persia to rule supreme and then the Greeks under the leadership of the young Alexander the Great, next the Romans, the European conquerors of indigenous peoples and so it continued and continues.

## The Gift of the Nile

During the building of a civilisation in Mesopotamia at the eastern end of the Fertile Crescent, another community of ancient people was creating its own great civilisation in Egypt to its western arc. The waters of the meandering Nile and the rich alluvial soil guiding its course to the Mediterranean Sea were the basis of Egyptian prosperity, the primary reason for the rise and growth of one of the most interesting classical civilisations our world has ever known. Herodotus, the Greek historian, described Egypt as 'the gift of the Nile' when he visited the country in 450 BCE. The Egyptians developed their own system of writing around 3,000 BCE. Instead of writing on clay tablets they created a material called 'papyrus' from papyrus reeds growing along the banks of the Nile. They regarded writing as 'the words of the gods'. For them it possessed a religious as well as a magical significance, a gift bestowed on them by Thoth, the god of wisdom.

The Egyptians worshipped as many as two thousand gods and goddesses (polytheism), in shrines, temples and in their homes. A temple was the earthly home of the god or goddess to whom it was dedicated. In it was housed a cult statue of the particular deity through which the spirit of the god or goddess was believed to communicate. Priests and priestesses tended the temples, praying over the offerings of the people. Ra was the sun god, Osiris the god of the Nile, Nut was the sky goddess, Isis, the patroness of crafts, Thoth, the god of wisdom, Anubis, the god of the dead and embalming and Hathor was goddess of love and beauty.

## The Lust for Immortality

The Egyptians believed that their kings or 'pharaohs' were gods, possessing supreme power and authority and ruling over their subjects from splendid palaces lavishly decorated with gold and precious stones. They had thousands of slaves at their command. They believed that death was a transitional stage on the journey to a more prosperous afterlife, the Next World, as they regarded it. They were convinced that life reached its full potential only after death, hence their care to ensure that the body survived intact. Their belief was that a person was composed of several elements, which were scattered in death. Reassembling these was vital to survival in the afterlife. As well as the body, which was one element, every person possessed a 'ka', or spirit, at birth, which accompanied them throughout their mortal existence. After death, it was important to make preparations to ensure that the ka did not leave them.

More than any other civilisation, the Egyptians were preoccupied with immortality. Burial was a ritual attended by family and friends and the survival of the dead depended on the goodwill of the living. Peasants and labourers had their eternal homes in sand holes. However, when a pharaoh died his body was embalmed, which took a few days, then wrapped in bandages with jewellery and amulets between the layers and finally covered with gold and precious stones before being laid in a coffin. The Egyptian kings, in an effort to preserve their bodies forever, had massive tombs erected for themselves and family members. Some of these were cut into cliffs in two remote valleys on the banks of the river Nile, lavishly decorated on the inside: the Valley of the Queens and the Valley of the Kings. Some were private tombs decorated with scenes from daily life to encourage the notion of the 'eternal home'. The pyramid-shaped tombs, introduced during the Old Kingdom, were the most spectacular of all. These were gigantic, impregnable tombs built by the people.

The Great Pyramid of Cheops at Giza, built for King Khufu and standing at one hundred and forty-six meters (480 feet) high, became known as one of the Seven Wonders of the World. One of the more interesting archaeological discoveries of the last century was that of Tutankamun, the Boy-Pharaoh's tomb, by British archaeologists Howard Carter and Lord Carnarvon. They uncovered the greatest collection of gold and jewellery ever seen. The tomb had three rooms furnished and decorated with precious stones, gold, statues, chariots as well as preserved food and wines.

## The Relentless Flow of Early Human Settlements
Far beyond the earliest settlements in the Middle East and Nile region, civilisations developed from small communities in the Indus Valley region of India and around the Yellow River in China. Little is known of these early settlers, but it is thought that they were mainly farmers and craftspeople. While the early Indus Valley civilisations completely disappeared and were forgotten under the rubble and the mists of time, the early farming cultures of China were succeeded by several dynasties. The Chinese believed that their rulers were descended from a god named Shang Ti. He alone possessed the power to grant the right to rule, a privilege that could be withdrawn at any time, hence the frequent change of dynasty in early Chinese history.

'A rich and lovely island, set in the wine-dark sea, densely peopled and boasting ninety cities'; this is how Homer described the island of Crete, south of mainland Greece in the Mediterranean Sea. Until its discovery by Sir Arthur Evans, Crete, home of king Minos, was considered a mythological place. Evans, an English archaeologist, brought to light an entire civilisation at the end of nineteenth century CE, one whose existence had never even been suspected. The people of Minoan Crete were the first civilisation in Europe. Here the seeds of Greek civilisation were sown. Minoan Crete, with its sophistication of palaces and luxurious surroundings, predated the emergence of classical Greek culture by over a thousand years.

The main religion of the Minoan period was centred on a mother goddess. She was worshipped in rock shelters and shrines from ancient times and before 1700 BCE people worshipped in mountain-top sanctuaries. The goddess was often depicted with symbols of living things: snakes, flowers and birds. The snake goddess was revered as a household guardian as depicted in a figure from Knossos, c. 1500 BCE. Offerings to the goddess were made in the form of clay models reflecting the worries and main concerns of the people. The bull, a recurring motif in Minoan art – frescos, buildings, and pottery – was a symbol of male potency. Religious ritual linking with the bull symbol gradually took the form of the worship of a young male god in the Minoan period.

What happened to this first flowering of civilisation in Europe? What forces could have silenced such a vivacious culture, blotting it out forever? Archaeology has revealed clues concerning a rich warrior culture on mainland Greece during the fifteenth century BCE. From Mycenae, bronze-clad warriors began to invade the isolated island. At about the same time Minoan Crete was gutted by a natural disaster, the second in its history; fire destroyed most of the settlements on the island with the exception of Knossos, which the Mycenaeans captured and restored.

Athens was one of the most famous cities in the world around 450 BCE as it emerged as the centre of Greek culture. People everywhere marvelled at the size and architectural beauty of its buildings. From high on a rock overlooking the city stood the Acropolis ('summit city'), surrounded by high walls with an imposing statue of the goddess Athene, for whom the city was named, adorning its centre. The Parthenon, a vast temple dedicated to Athene Parthenos ('the Virgin Athene'), dominated the Acropolis. Situated beneath the Acropolis was the Agora, or market place, of Athens where merchants traded their wares, people gathered to discuss business and politics and where slaves were bought and sold. Adjoining the marbled magnificence of the Acropolis and Agora, houses and workshops of neighbouring streets were small and constructed of mud walls.

The Mediterranean world, between 700 and 300 BCE, was a powerful player in the shaping of western civilisation. The impact of Classical Greek ideas on philosophy, science, literature, art and architecture endures to the present. Athens was the home of Plato, Sophocles and Euripides. Greek civilisation developed around the *polis,* or city-state. These independent, self-governing communities were characterised by walled cities with outlying villages and farms. It has been the general belief over the centuries that government by the people began in Athens. This is not quite accurate since women and slaves were excluded from the Assembly, which governed affairs. What about the much earlier roots and flowering of democracy in matrilineal societies and in Sumer? Can we keep confining these to the mists of time even amid growing archaeological evidence? Similar forgetfulness occurred in more recent times when the Iroquois roots of American democracy were confined to the shadow of the Founding Fathers. How our world today needs the Iroquois Great Law of Peace with its emphasis on individual liberty, justice, freedom of speech, religion and the right of women to participate in politics and governance.

However, the classical Greek form of democratic government was to have profound implications for the world at large, particularly through the conquests of Philip of Macedon and his son Alexander III of Macedon, better known as Alexander the Great. By the time of Alexander's death at the age of thirty-two, his conquests in toppling the mighty Persians had extended Greek influence into Egypt, Mesopotamia, Hindu Kush and India's western borders. His enduring contribution lay in opening up new horizons, in bringing different people and cultural traditions together and establishing trade routes linking the Mediterranean with India, Asia and East Africa.

Rome, the eternal city and capital of Italy, was for some eight hundred years (from c. 400 BCE), the hub of the powerful Roman Empire. Around two thousand years ago, Rome was the largest, most magnificent and busiest place in the world. The ancient Romans loved to relax in huge public baths, the most famous being the Baths of Diocletian and Caracalla. These resembled mini-cities with libraries, restaurants and shops. The Romans built huge aqueducts; these stone arches supplied the city with water from the neighbouring hills. Rome was at the height of its power during the first and second centuries CE, defeating the Greeks and controlling all of Italy and huge swathes of Europe. The vast empire extended from Britain in the north to Egypt and North Africa in the south and from Iberia in the west as far eastward as the Persian Gulf. Italy adopted Christianity after the conversion of the Roman Emperor Constantine in 313 CE.

## A Colourful Tapestry

The geographical composition of the Roman Empire rendered it impossible to have one set of mythological and religious traditions. As it expanded its territories, it incorporated the religious beliefs and ritual expressions of these people into its own. This wove a colourful tapestry of Greek, Egyptian and Celtic strands besides some uniquely Roman highlights. The Egyptian goddess, Isis, goddess of fertility and crafts, was introduced into Italy (second century BCE), she became popular and was sometimes associated with Fortuna, the Roman goddess of love, fertility and agriculture. Perhaps the most extraordinary deity introduced to Rome was Cybele, the 'Great Mother' or 'Magma Mater' from Phrygia.

The Greek pantheon of gods and goddesses was assimilated into the Roman one. Mount Olympus, the highest mountain in Greece was thought to be the home of the principal deities. Zeus was regarded as the father of the gods, whose dominion was the sky. He had two brothers, Poseidon, who ruled the sea and Hades, the sovereign ruler of the underworld. Athene, the wise one, goddess of Athens and patron of crafts was the daughter of Zeus and Metis. With the goddess Demeter, Zeus fathered Persephone, who became goddess of the Underworld. Apollo, the god of music and poetry and his sister, the goddess Artemis, the virgin huntress, were children of

Zeus. Zeus' other daughter, Aphrodite, goddess of love, beauty and fertility, is alleged to have sprung from the foaming sea.

The Roman equivalent of Zeus was Jupiter, of Athene, Minerva, of Artemis, Diana, of Poseidon, Neptune, of Aphrodite, Venus, and so forth. Demeter, the goddess of corn, vegetation and abundance (Roman, Ceres), was central to the important cult of Eleusis, near Athens, where her mysterious powers of growth and resurrection were celebrated annually in the autumn. This Bronze Age mystery-religion of the Greeks manifested a shift in consciousness from the visible, tangible world to a deep, eternal aspect. The story of Demeter and her daughter, Persephone, has very ancient roots; it is a powerful myth that personifies growth and decay and is associated with a dying and reviving deity. The Eleusis festivities recalled the loss of her daughter, Persephone, to Hades and the Underworld and her rediscovery at the intervention of her father, Zeus.

In some versions of the myth Zeus was responsible for her 'marriage' to Hades in the first instance; other versions tell us that Hades stole her away and tricked her into eating his food). Demeter, which means 'mother earth', lost all interest in fertility during Persephone's abduction to the Underworld. Consequently, all plants withered and died and animals ceased to multiply. When Zeus finally intervened, an arrangement was made whereby Persephone would divide her time equally between her mother and her husband, hence the seasons of spring and autumn. This powerful myth has informed other cultures and religious traditions.[6]

It was at the time of Roman sovereignty that the idea of the 'heroic' warrior became popular. The one who sacrificed himself/herself for the sake of the country or empire became the one to emulate. This is highlighted by the Roman poet, Virgil, in his epic poem, *The Aeneid*, about the Trojan hero, Aeneas, son of Venus, the goddess of love. In Rome, patriarchy – a system in society whereby males hold the power with the male being head, and descent reckoned through the male line – reached its peak. Male domination had been growing with the rise of the city state cultures, which were ruled by kings or powerful warlords: Babylon, Persia, Egypt, India, China and Greece. From about 800 BCE, while the great Greek goddesses were widely honoured in shrines and temples, women were relegated to second-class citizenry, excluded from public office and rendered subservient to fathers, husbands and brothers. When the Emperor, Constantine, and his subjects throughout the Roman Empire converted to Christianity from 313 CE, the final demise of the goddesses was imminent. The Christian era ushered in the leadership of emperors, kings, bishops and popes. There was an initial short period of relative gender equality soon to be side-lined by the Church's male hierarchy, a situation, which sadly persists to the present day.

One could be forgiven for assuming that the entire human family was accounted for in the magnitude and magnificence of the leading civilisation centres referred to above. The reality, however, is quite the opposite with larger regions of the planet like sub-Saharan Africa, Australia, the South Pacific, North America, South America and some inner regions of Eurasia, remaining beyond their boundary of influence. These were home to multitudes of indigenous peoples.

Before the European incursions and conquests of the late fifteenth century, Central and North America had remained relatively isolated from the rest of the inhabited world. Since the emergence of village life, the earliest complex settlements were established near Gautemala south of the Gulf of Mexico. The Olmec civilisation, perhaps the mother culture of Central America, developed around 1150 BCE. They had kings and class systems, traded widely and fought many wars. They were skilled builders, worked in ceramics, stone and jewels. The Olmecs established the Mesoamerican pantheon of gods as well as the syllabary writing system.

It was south of the Yucatan that the Mayan civilisation began as early as 1,000 BCE. The terrain, a combination of highland and lowland, was important to trade within the Mayan civilisation. The lowlands produced a variety of crops such as maize, squash, chilli peppers, beans, cacao, cotton and sisal while the volcanic highlands were a source of obsidian, jade and other precious metals. The great river networks were vital in transportation and trade. Similar to the Greeks, the Mayan peoples were both religiously and artistically a nation, but politically sovereign city-states. The Classic Mayan civilisation is regarded as the first fully literate culture of the Americas; they had developed a hieroglyphic writing system. Tikal was the axis of human affairs, the centre of economic life, of commerce and trade and above all the place where the mysteries of creation, of life and death were ritually acknowledged.

The Valley of Mexico was already highly urbanised when the Aztecs entered it around 1200 CE. Most of their settlements were on the shores of the magnificent Lake Texcoco and it was here that they established their renowned capital Tenochtitlan. This is the site of Mexico City today. Tenochtitlan ('the place of the cactus'), became the capital of the Aztec Empire in 1428 with a population of over three hundred thousand, the heart of an empire with up to ten million people. The god of rain and abundant harvest, Tlaloc, was central to Aztec belief and the god of war and the sun was regarded as the protector of the Aztec people. The Spanish conquest of the sixteenth century saw the substitution of Christianity for the Native Indian religions and the forced imposition of Spanish rule throughout Central America. The battles against the Aztec were actually won not so much by the invading Spaniards under Hernan Cortes as by the tens of thousands of Indian allies. Sadly it was a decisive Indian victory over Indians.

The Inca Empire (1438-1532) emerged as the most prominent state in South America and ruled with total power and control for almost a century. The Inca society was hierarchical, the rulers believing that they were descended from the sun. Cuzco, the Inca City of the Sun, was the site where the divine and human communicated with each other, where life's mysteries were shared and relationships reconciled. The Inca crumbled, already vulnerable with internal crises, before the mighty Spanish *conquistadors*, under Pizarro in 1532.

## Reserved Wisdom

In 1998, while studying in the United States, I had the privilege of living for a short period on a Reservation in Montana and participating in the life of the Northern Cheyenne and Crow Peoples. Walking the scorched earth under a 'big' sky, sharing food, ideas, hopes and frustrations with people, and particularly through participating in their sacred ceremonies, has rendered me a much more alive, cosmic citizen and a more contrite, humble European. In light of that conversion experience, I can more easily imagine what life must have been like for the indigenous peoples of the world before the bloody conquests and ruthless uprooting by people regarded as civilised, which have resulted in the inhumane confinement to reservation areas today. I can picture the wide-open spaces, the echoes of silence, the myriad voices communicating with each other and other beings in the family of creation, the music in the wind, rocks, trees and seas mingling with the dance, laughter, the tears, joys and sorrows of people intimate with the Earth and her bountifulness. Our world will never again experience such diversity of language, customs, dance and song, arts and poetry, music and religious ceremony. What have we lost forever? What lessons might we learn with regard to the whole community of life?

## The Weaving of Classical Religions

The establishment of organised religions was connected to the growth of urban civilisations. From these early civilisations certain common characteristics began to emerge from the lived experience of people, their beliefs in the face of ultimate mystery, their mythology and wealth of ritual expression. The early emergence of a priestly class particularly from the shamanic tradition – as in Sumer – in the practice of sacrifice and offerings to the gods, ancestor worship and especially the spiritual consciousness manifested in burial practices formed the core elements of organised religion. Hinduism has its roots in Vedism, the religion of the ancient Aryan tribes (Indo-European), who inhabited northern India during the second millennium BCE. The sacred texts of Hinduism are the Vedas, which highlight the roles of various Hindu gods and goddesses in the functioning of the universe and the place of the human in the cosmic order. There is a deep sense of identity between the human and the natural world in Hinduism, a compassion for every living being.

Judaism originated around 1,200 BCE as a tribal religion of people tracing their ancestry back to Abraham, in Mesopotamia, their exile in Egypt and Exodus to the Promised Land. Judaism remained unique in being monotheistic, worshipping Yahweh, the One God. King David formalised it as a state religion of Israel c. 1,000 BCE. Although it has a comparatively small following today (c. 14 million), it holds a place at the centre of western civilisation, strongly influencing the systems of law, economics, education, politics and religion throughout the Western World. It is also significant for its age and vibrant culture, and as the seedbed of Christianity and Islam. Christianity took root as a movement within Judaism. The central doctrine is the belief in Jesus Christ, the Son of God, the Messiah prophesied in the Old Testament. Jesus was crucified and rose from the dead as testified by the apostles, his followers, and preached throughout the Mediterranean. The Christian message spread throughout the expanse of the Roman Empire, meeting persecution by the Romans and eventual adoption as the state religion with the conversion of Constantine in 313 CE.

The prophet Muhammad, a merchant from Mecca in Arabia, founded Islam early in the seventh century CE. His regard for the Judaeo-Christian prophets, including Jesus Christ, was influential in that he regarded them as forerunners of Islam. He received revelations concerning the worship of the one God ('Allah') and set about preaching particularly against the polytheistic practices in his homeland. Like the early Christians, he met with persecution and had to flee to Medina in 622 CE. By the time of his death ten years later he had gained the political and spiritual leadership of much of Arabia. After his death, Islam spread far beyond the confines of Arabia, to Spain and Morocco, to central Asia and Afghanistan.

Buddhism, like Christianity and Islam is a proselytising religion. It is based on the enlightenment experienced by one man, Siddhartha Gautama. He lived in north-eastern India in the sixth century BCE. He sought enlightenment, which he received through meditation, thus becoming the Buddha, the 'Awakened One'. Elimination of the self is the route to enlightenment. The final goal of the Buddhist is *nirvana*, the transcendent state of bliss. The religion founded by the Buddha was in many ways a reaction to the excesses of Aryan religious practices. The idea that compassion due to humans ought to be extended to other forms of life is strong in Buddhism. The Buddha travelled India as an itinerant preacher for over forty years before formalising his religious beliefs. His teachings spread into southern Asia, to Japan, Tibet and China.

Taoism developed in China during the Zhou dynasty. It became the most widespread of all Chinese religions. Worship was centred on ancestors, sacred places and spirits in nature. A prophet named Lao-tzu codified this religion. He taught that correct behaviour in people would result from being in tune with the natural world. In the sixth century BCE, a prophet named Kong Zi, known in the West as Confucius, lived in a time of chronic warfare in China. He believed that peace could only prevail if people were to obey a strict code of behaviour. This later formed the basis of Chinese social and political conduct.

It is interesting to note that Buddhism, Confucianism, and later, Christianity, became world religions through being adopted by powerful political rulers, who ensured their promotion, sometimes even by force. Throughout recorded history politics and religion have indeed soldiered together. Classical religious traditions have contributed enormously, especially by way of acknowledging the individual and one's relationship with God, whoever God might be for each one. They have afforded stability, solace, peace of mind and community support to millions. However, one is compelled to ask: what have they – singly and collectively – done to women? The sort of discrimination that systematically excludes women (at present, more than half of the world's population) must surely call into question the credibility of their core message.

It is true to say that most organised religions have, individually and collectively, been at best lukewarm in their relationship with the sacred community, which is the universe. Within these traditions, there developed a deep distrust of the natural world. Earth came to be seen as a transition place on the way to eternity. Although God was believed to have created everything, yet it was considered necessary to transcend created things in order to be with God. Perhaps it is time, as Anne Primavesi advocates, to see planet Earth once more as a heavenly body. To acknowledge that we are Earthlings and that God is nearer to us than we are to ourselves every single moment of every day.

## Our Lost Psychic Heritage

Preserved in a cave sanctuary for over twenty thousand years, a female figure speaks to us about the minds of our early Western ancestors. She is small and carved out of stone: one of the so-called Venus figurines found all over prehistoric Europe.[7]

What sort of people were our goddess-worshipping predecessors? How arrogant are we in determining what ought to be defined as history? Are there perhaps jewels of wisdom from our early cultural evolution that need to be accorded the light of day and polished to sparkle with counsel in out time? While there are no written records before c. 3,000 BCE, two dating methods essential to the chronology of earlier millennia are helping archaeologists and cultural historians. These are radiocarbon, or carbon 14, and dendrochronology or tree-ring counting. These methods together with the discoveries and writings of such eminent scholars as: Marija Gimbutas, Riane Eisler, Joseph Campbell, James Mellaart, Arthur Evans and Charlene Spretnak are helping to push the historical and cultural boundaries further and further back in time.

Ever since the dawn of human emergence, our earliest ancestors communicated using visual signs and symbols etched on the landscape to convey meaning and information. Since about 8,000 BCE, Near Eastern communities used clay shapes or tokens in trading transactions. Geometric designs represented measures of grain or individual animals and as village settlements emerged around 4,000 BCE, the tokens were shaped to resemble the commodities they represented. The early Europeans (c. 7,000-3,500 BCE), initiated rather complex social organisation which required craft specialisation. They created religious and governmental institutions of a complex nature. They were adept copper and gold smiths in the creation of ornaments, jewellery and tools. They possessed a rudimentary script form as well as elaborate artistic abilities, especially in pottery, painting and weaving. European archaeologist, Marija Gimbutas, makes the observation:

> If one defines civilization as the ability of a given people to adjust to its environment and to develop adequate arts, technology, script, and social relationships, it is evident that Old Europe achieved a marked degree of success.[8]

Gimbutas refers to Old Europe and Indo-Europe, the former characterised as a matrilineal society (descent and inheritance traced through the mother) with egalitarian female-male structures and predominantly peaceful. The latter, whom she terms the Kurgan (Indo-European) invaders from the Northern Steppes, form a male-dominated, hierarchical (ranking system according to given status or authority) and warfaring society. She is adamant that the idea of warfare as endemic to the human condition is a gross misunderstanding and rejects the assumption that civilisation refers only to androcratic (male-dominated) warrior societies:

> In creating a situation in which they could nurture and rear infants safely and affectively, women became the civilisers, the inventors of agriculture, of community, some maintain of language itself.[9]

The result of the clash of Old European with alien Indo-European religious forms and symbolisms became visible in the ousting of old European goddesses, shrines and sacred symbols. This occurred initially in east-central Europe and soon spread to all of central Europe. However, Crete and the

Aegean Islands, together with central and western Mediterranean areas, continued Old European traditions for several millennia more before succumbing to the might of warrior gods. The core of the civilisation was lost, but the ancient images and symbols could not be totally uprooted from the human psyche. The goddess religion, wherein there was no separation between the sacred and secular – religion was life, and life was religion – was forced underground or became assimilated into Indo-European ideology.

## Celtic Roots

The Celts, a farming and warlike people, were the first Indo-European people to spread across Europe. They left no written records since they relied exclusively on the spoken word and trained memories. What we know of them comes mainly from the writings of Greeks and Romans as well as the records of early Christian monks in Ireland. This written information is supplemented by archaeological discoveries of the Hallstatt Culture (discovered in Austria in 1846) and La Tene Culture (discovered in Switzerland in 1858). They were farmers and traders with defined societal patterns rivalling in opulence and grandeur of civilisation their Iron Age counterparts among the later Greeks and Romans. Between c. 1,300 and 400 BCE the Celts spread throughout most of Europe. Their power was augmented by their use of iron, a new and stronger metal. It is believed that the Celts came to Ireland around 600 BCE. They brought new customs, expertise and skills as well as their own language, tools and weaponry. Like the Greeks and Romans, the Celts worshipped a variety of gods and goddesses, including ones sacred to the people they conquered as we shall see when exploring our ancient, pre-Celtic roots.

## Traces in the Sand

Have you ever wondered while enjoying the beauty and diversity of Ireland who might have been the first people to embrace this land? Who would have composed the community of beings – flora, fauna and elements – forming the welcoming party?

These were the hazel, pine, juniper, elm, oak, birch, crab apple, grasses, docks and meadowsweet. Animals would have included the wild pig, red deer and the hare, while the melody of birdsong would have come from the song-thrush, coot, wood pigeon, golden eagle, red grouse, widgeon, snipe and mallard. The rivers and sea provided their particular hospitality with salmon, trout, plaice, flounder, eels and a variety of shellfish. Could it have been that the earliest footprints were on cooler earth, fresh from melting ice as the glaciers retreated during one of the warmer phases of the Old Stone Age some fifteen to twenty thousand years ago? This was the glorious period of the wondrous cave paintings in France and Spain. This seems more and more unlikely as archaeologists generally agree that human occupation is post-glacial, after 9,000 BCE. What would have attracted the first settlers? Perhaps it was by chance that this tiny island tucked away in the North-Western corner of Europe was among the last of the European countries to be inhabited.

Is it possible that the first people came to Ireland via one or more of the land bridges still linking Ireland and Britain about nine thousand years ago? Alternatively, they may have arrived by boat via Britain or France. The Irish countryside was for the most part under dense forest cover therefore people tended to settle near rivers and lakes using small boats made from animal hides as means of transport. Excavation work by Peter Woodman in 1970s and 1980s at Mount

Sandel in Co. Derry, overlooking the river Bann, has revolutionised opinions on the Mesolithic Period in Ireland. His work revealed a settlement of perhaps fifteen people whose houses are the oldest Mesolithic ones to be discovered in Ireland and pre-date any so far found in Britain. The houses had hearths and remains of simple cooking structures. These hunter-gatherers used small flint points and axes. Many miles away in a large area of raised bog, known as Boora Bog, near Tullamore, Co. Offaly, excavations carried out by the National Museum of Ireland unearthed a settlement largely similar and roughly contemporary with Mount Sandel.

The forested landscape remained almost unaltered until the arrival of the first farmers heralding the emergence of the Neolithic culture (New Stone Age) from the Eurasian landmass around 4,000 BCE. As in the Fertile Crescent, so too in Ireland, the farming and domestication of animals were to transform the Irish environment forever. The forests were the first to feel the impact of these new settlers, as land was cleared to grow crops and rear animals for hunting, protection, food, clothing and shelter. The people brought with them already advanced skills such as pottery, weaving and architecture. We know that crops of barley and wheat were cultivated extensively from pottery impressions. The recovery of bones reveals the presence of cattle and sheep as well as dogs and horses. Remains of axe factories show the widespread use of stone in axe making and polishing. The discovery of Neolithic houses associated with field systems or enclosures gives us a glimpse of what life was like. Among the most spectacular examples are: Ceide Fields, Co. Mayo, Lough Gur, Co. Limerick and Malinmore, Co. Donegal.

The relationship of these early inhabitants with their dead tells us most about their beliefs and skills. The Irish countryside, notwithstanding the rapacious Celtic Tiger, still houses many great stone burial chambers, testimony to the hopes, dreams, prayers and very bones of our ancestors. Lough Gur, Co.Limerick, is a magnificent example of a Neolithic settlement (c. 3000 BCE) with over thirty ancient sites and monuments, including stone circles, standing stones, megalithic tombs and family dwellings. The three most common burial monuments in Ireland during the Neolithic Period were the court, portal and passage tombs numbering over 1,200 sites of varying size and magnificence. The former two predominate north of a line running from Galway to Dundalk. The latter have a tendency to cluster in 'cemetery' form, for example, The Boyne Valley: Newgrange, Dowth, Knowth, Loughcrew (Co. Meath) and Carrowmore, Co. Sligo.

During the Bronze Age in Ireland (c. 2,000-500 BCE), the most common type of burial chamber used was the wedge tomb, a rectangular structure, narrower and lower towards the back. Wedge tombs are more widely scattered than any other form with many occurring in Munster where other types are rare. The Bronze Age was the period of stone circles with over two hundred and forty of them distributed throughout Ireland, mainly in mid-Ulster and Southwest Munster.[10] These circles of standing stones were probably connected with religious ceremonies such as worship of the Sun, which was revenced by our ancestors as vital for life and sustenance.

### From the Mists of Eternity

What did our earliest Irish ancestors look like? Where did they come from? Who and how did they worship? Mythological stories were transmitted orally from the earliest settlers around 7,000 BCE until 1,000 CE. Irish scholars compiled written manuscripts in the eleventh and twelfth centuries CE. This work is known as The Book of Invasions and gives us valuable information regarding history and precious mythology. In the western world particularly there has been a strong tendency to relegate myth to the realm of the unreal and therefore miss out on its mystical influence. This is partly due, according to early Irish historian, Brother Paulinus MacTomais, to the power of the Greek Sophists in the fifth century BCE. They toppled *'muthos'* meaning 'word' or 'speech' implying reflection or pondering from its central position and replaced it with *'logos'* implying abstract thought and debate. Both of these are important, it is not 'either-or', but a balance of both. There is more to our experience than can be defined or categorised, the invisible beyond the visible, which is core to spirituality.

The original inhabitants of Ireland seem to have been a thin, small, black-haired people with sallow skin, probably akin to the Basques of the Pyrenees in northern Spain. We do not know what became of these earliest ancestors. Did they return to mainland Europe or did they die out as a race on Irish soil? There is no conclusive evidence regarding this. The Book of Invasions describes subsequent invasions as follows:

  ❧ *c.*2,200 BCE *The Parthalonians* who came to Ireland from Macedonia by way of Iberia. They were a giant race, but were apparently totally wiped out by famine and pestilence after three hundred years.

  ❧ *c.* 2,000 BCE *The Nemedians,* followers of Nemidus, from Greece or the Balkans. After two hundred years they were largely wiped out in battle with the Formorians. It is related that this battle was fought 'with savage fierceness' near Lough Swilly, in Inishowen, Co. Donegal.

✥ c. 1800 BCE *The Formorians*, reputed to have been a ruthless, sea-roving people from Africa, who had a stronghold on Tory Island, on the North West coast of Donegal. They seem to have plundered rather than settled on the land.

✥ c. 1700 BCE *The Firbolgs*, a dark-haired and intelligent race with a pastoral background from the eastern Mediterranean. They divided Ireland into five provinces: Ulster, Munster, Connacht and Leinster, with the area around Mullingar, Co. Westmeath in the centre of the country, known as Uisneach. These provinces remain the same today except for the fifth province, the territory of which became incorporated into Leinster. The fifth province remains a powerful symbol of imagination, creativity and unity in a politically divided land.

✥ c. 1600 BCE *The Tuatha De Danaans*, meaning the skilled workers, who are believed to have come from the River Elbe region of Germany, but were actually the direct descendants of the earlier Nemedians. Nemedius' grandson had left Ireland with his family to escape the Formorians; they had settled in the northern islands of Greece. Legend tells us they attacked Scotland en route, but hastened to Ireland, which they claimed rightly belonged to them. It is believed that the impressive ring fort at Grianan of Aileach (Co. Donegal) was erected during the reign of their king, Dagda. It was from a De Danaan queen, named Ériu, that Ireland derived its name (Erin). The De Danaans are associated with the worship of the goddess Danu, who like Ériu and Brigit, was known as a triple goddess – maiden, mother and crone – who connected with the wisdom and playfulness of the underworld in trying to build bridges across all divides.

❧ *c.* 1,500 BCE *The Milesians,* from Spain, who took over the government of the country from the Tuatha De Danaan. This was the coming of the Gaels to Ireland. Legend has it that even though the Tuatha De Danaan were defeated in battle, they still managed to retain their supernatural powers and magical skills and they continued to make life difficult for the newcomers until a truce was made between them. It was agreed to divide the country between them, the territory underground to belong to the Tuatha De Danaan and the land above ground to the Milesians. And so the Tuatha retired to live underground, the Dagda, their king, gave a *'sidh'* or fairy mound, to each of their chieftains and ever afterwards these mounds were to be the dwellings of the fairy folk, the 'wee folk' of Ireland. Whatever the view of this agreement, it is true that for generations certain areas of land and particular trees, regarded in oral tradition to be sacred to the fairies, would be left untouched by farmers and builders lest some misfortune might befall the family or community.[11]

## Ancient Threads of Irish Spirituality

Like the early civilisations in Mesopotamia, Egypt, China, India, Greece and Rome, ancient Irish peoples worshipped many goddesses and gods. The mysteries of life and afterlife created the impression that there were hidden forces in the environment. There was the widespread belief, often ritualised, that spirits inhabited the earth, sea and sky. Many of the deities of ancient Ireland were adopted by the Celts when they arrived c. 500 BCE thus making it difficult to distinguish what existed among the primal inhabitants. Anu (Danu, Dana) was the mother goddess of Irish mythology. The Tuatha De Danaan ('the people of the goddess Danu') were her divine offspring, these were the gods and goddesses ruling Ireland before the arrival of the Milesians. Boann, the goddess of water (river Boyne named after her) was the mother of Aonghus, the god of love. His father was Dagda, the father of the gods and one of the Tuatha De Danaan.

Brigit (Brigid), the goddess of healing and fertility was the wife of Bres, who briefly led the Tuatha De Danaan after the first battle with the Firbolgs. It is thought that Brigid or Bride, the Christian saint, may have been Brigit or a priestess of the goddess Brigit before her conversion to Christianity. Ériu, goddess of fire and the hearth, and her two sisters – Banba and Fodla – were of the Tuatha De Danaan. Lugh, son of Balor of Formorian origin, was the Celtic sun god. Macha was an Irish war goddess, associated with her were Morrigan, Badb and Nemain. Oisín, who tasted the Salmon of Knowledge and often regarded as the greatest poet in Ireland, was the son of the goddess Badb and Finn MacCool, High King of Ireland.

When Constantine, emperor of the Roman Empire, adopted Christianity in 313 CE this became the official religion of the Roman territories. Roman forces advancing west as far as Britain never entered Ireland, the country lay outside the confines of the mighty Empire. It was over one hundred years later before Christianity took hold in Ireland through the missionary journeys of St Patrick, and later under the influence of St Brigid, and then the monastic settlements throughout the country. The Christian faith in the one God, incarnated in Jesus Christ, became the official religion even though reverence and respect for the former goddesses and gods continued as we know from the profusion of holy wells, streams, sacred trees and hallowed places around the country to this day: 'Some of the saints have clearly succeeded pre-Christian deities in the task of presiding over wells and other sacred sites.'[12]

## Notes

1. *The Little Book of Native American Wisdom*, 10, (Element Books Ltd. Great Britain, USA and Australia, 1994).
2. *The Message of the Myth Part 11* in 'The Power of Myth' by Joseph Campbell (Mystic Fire Video Inc., Netherlands, 1988).
3. *Vanished Civilisations*, 14, (The Reader's Digest Association Limited, London, 2002).
4. Ibid. 19.
5. *The Universe Story* eds., Brian Swimme & Thomas Berry, 185, (HarperSanFrancisco, 1992).
6. Information on the goddesses and gods from *The Ultimate Encyclopedia of Mythology* by Arthur Cotterell & Rachel Storm (Lorenz Books, London, 1999); *World Mythology* Arthur Cotterell (Paragon Books, UK, 2000) and *The Sacred Isle* by Daithí O'Hogain (Collins Press, Cork, 1999).
7. *The Chalice and the Blade* by Riane Eisler, 1, (HarperSanFrancisco, 1987).
8. *The Goddesses and Gods of Old Europe*, 7000-3500 BC Marija Gimbutas, 17, (Berkeley and Los Angeles: University of California Press, 1982).
9. *The Civilisation of the Goddess: The World of Old Europe* by Marija Gimbutas (Harper, 1991).

10. See *Out of Fire* above.
11. Much of the information in this section is taken from *Druids, Gods, and Heroes from Celtic Mythology* by Anne Ross (Peter Bedrick Books, New York, 1994, and *Romantic Stories and Legends of Donegal* Harry Swan (W.J. Barr & Sons, Donegal, Ireland, 1969). Recommended further reading: *From the First Setttler to the Celts* by Peter Harbison (Thames & Hudson, 1988); *Reading the Irish Landscape* Frank Mitchell & Michael Ryan (Town House, Dublin, Ireland, 1986) and *Ancient Ireland* Laurence Flanagan (Gill & MacMillan, 1998).
12. *Fishstonewater: Holy Wells of Ireland* by Anna Rackard, Liam O'Callaghan, Angela Bourke (Atrium, Cork, Ireland, 2001).

# OUT OF ESTRANGEMENT & DOMINANCE

## An Invitation to Come Home

From where I stand the sea is just a rumour.
The stars are put out by our streetlamp. Light
And seawater are well separated.
                    Eavan Boland
                    (from 'Our Origins Are In The Sea')

Our family homestead in Inishowen, Co. Donegal, lies within earshot of the mighty Atlantic Ocean. I vividly recall winter nights being lulled to sleep by the dancing waves as they circled Inistrahull Island before foaming into the rugged face of Malin Head. The distant tone of the foghorn gradually receded as my head sank into my pillow of dreams. My parents were rooted in the land and as children we grew up within a wide and varied community of life. Animals – domesticated and free roaming – insects, birds, fish, trees, hedgerows, grassland, bogland, several plant species as well as flowers and fruit shared life with us. The mountains and hills, the valleys and extensive waterways in the bioregion of Inishowen,[1] situated between Lough Swilly and Lough Foyle, encircled us.

## A Child Remembers

In those childhood days, just before the widespread introduction of mechanised agriculture, farming was a family and wider community affair. As my father turned the first sod of earth in spring with his horse-drawn plough, he was making food available not only to us his family, but also to the birds, insects and other animals in the community of life. In the warm, moist exposed soil teeming with life some beings were becoming food for others in the cycle of life. This miracle of mutual nourishment had been initiated about 2 billion years ago through the process of photosynthesis. We too were an integral part of that process as we gave of our energy, time, perspiration and aching limbs often in harsh weather conditions. There was fun and sport too with a profound sense of togetherness both as people and as the living countryside. The absolute miracle of the Sun as the source of life is something that I have learned about scientifically in recent years, but I knew it intuitively from my parents and extended family since childhood. Through their intimacy with the Sun and the night sky, as indicated earlier, they were able to forecast the weather and mark the time with remarkable accuracy. They sensed the mystery of life and reverenced God, the Creator of all.

## Holy Ground

'Is maith an scealai an aimsir', 'Time is a great storyteller'. The evolutionary story of the human is a very impressive one. It began potentially with the flaring forth of the original fireball over 13 billion years ago. Between 2 and 7 million years ago our forebears came down from the trees and began roaming the wide, open spaces of the planet and then decided to cluster together in farming communities, known as the

Neolithic villages. From these a portion of the population gradually fashioned the major civilisations and cities of the world together with the great religious traditions. We have this ancestral inheritance in every cell of our bodies. What wisdom, inventiveness, heroism, sense of wonder and compassion will this evoke in us as we endeavour to enhance the quality of life not only for ourselves but also for future generations of the entire community of life? The powerful attraction of the Neolithic village is obvious when one considers that by 1800 CE there were fewer than three per cent of the population living in an urban context. By 1900 this figure had risen to around ten per cent.[2] Even in modern times, with huge urban sprawls, home to some two and a half billion people and rising steadily, we have the example of the vast subcontinent of India, the second most populous country in the world with almost 1 billion people. It has a scattering of urban centres in a vast network of over six hundred thousand villages, surely a legacy of Gandhi's ideal of village self-sufficiency. The landscape of China still displays a huge number of villages, as do many parts of Africa and South America. Ireland remained largely rural until the closing quarter of the twentieth century. Indigenous communities throughout the world remain in close contact with the Earth.

I believe that the enduring success of the Neolithic village lifestyle is directly linked to the attitude to the land. As we become more estranged from the land, particularly through the need to dominate the processes of food production to satiate the market economy, it is inevitable that populations become more and more displaced and the drift to urban centres intensifies. It is predicted that by 2030 up to sixty per cent of the world's people will be living in cities. In 1970, for example, there were three mega-cities (in excess of 10 million inhabitants) and by 1990 this number almost reached twenty. According to John Reader writing in the *Guardian* recently: 'By 2020 at least twenty-three cities will have passed the 10 million mark and nearly six hundred cities will have a million or more inhabitants'.[3] The most dramatic increase is predicted for the developing world. My question is: 'How much is the crowding into cities a matter of choice or of expediency?' It is alarming to note that one of the most fertile lands on the planet, the United States of America, now has more prisoners than farmers.[4]

The lure of urban convenience, the possibilities in terms of work, shopping, recreation, cultural life and the buzz characteristic of cities generally attract many people to cities. However, I do believe that there are many, specifically those ruthlessly uprooted from their lands and livelihoods in the name of so-called progress in our multi-national and global market driven economy, who would prefer to live on the land. This is becoming equally the pattern with regard to small businesses in towns and villages. The way that our global economy is structured is rendering the small enterprise increasingly untenable.

According to Helena Norberg-Hodge, 'as the effects of economic policies that ignore the needs of people and the planet become glaringly apparent, rebuilding community and local economies becomes more and more urgent'.[5] Helena is one of the pioneers of the Ecovillage movement, which has been developing in the industrialised west over the past thirty years. The first Ecovillage initiated in Ireland was established in Cloughjordan, Co. Tipperary in 1999. Individuals and families are coming together to build an Ecovillage future, whereby they nurture more intimate relations among people and encourage deeper connection and responsibility to the natural world. These villages are built with eco-friendly and sustainable materials and the inhabitants engage in environmentally healthy and sustainable sources of livelihood.

## Soil Mates

The soil with its powers of creativity and regeneration, the wonder of seeds, is an embodiment of the mystery of life. The land – soil – is not a commodity, a machine that produces food when pumped with fertiliser. It is rather a partner evoking reverence and respect, a eucharistic banquet inviting the whole community of life to be nourished and replenished and in turn to respect and nurture one another. When one considers that it can take up to a thousand years to create an inch of topsoil it is alarming how billions of tons of it are being washed away, particularly as a result of destructive farming methods and deforestation.[6] Topsoil, rich in organic matter and billions of living organisms, is like the skin of the Earth. Just as nutritionists and health and beauty experts advise us that our skin, the body's largest organ, reveals the overall health of our bodies and that it must be nourished and replenished so that we glow with vitality, so too with the face of the Earth.

There is an ever-widening chasm between the rich natural properties in the soil through the conscientious work of billions of tiny microbes with the need for fallow time and the monotony of mono-cultural cash cropping. The living soil partnered our early ancestors as they learned the art of horticulture. They knew that the soil had to be fed with the waste products of plants, animals and humans and that the tiny micro-organisms did the rest as they laboured in their billions beneath our feet. Humans soon discovered that co-operating with Nature's creative processes yielded the best results. Earthworms are one of Nature's best recyclers; they impressed Aristotle, who hailed them as the intestines of the Earth. They pass the soil through their bodies, gradually, converting decaying organic matter into humus. The soil is aerated and enriched as up to twenty tons of soil per acre are churned to the surface every year thereby maintaining a healthy texture and fertility.

Earthworms are assisted in their underground movement by thousands of small animals (snails, millipedes, springtails, eelworms) and at the microscopic level by billions of bacteria, fungi and moulds. What an incredible community enterprise! It is amazing to think that there are more bacteria in a teaspoonful of healthy soil than there are people on planet Earth, and we are currently in excess of six billion.[7] To add to this amazing fact, Liz Sheppard, in her book *Donegal for All Seasons*, intrigues us: 'Next time you see a field full of grazing cattle, here's a thought worth pondering: the total weight of the animals on the surface is considerably less than the weight of earthworms underneath!'[8]

## Changing Relations

The cultivation of the land together with the domestication of animals from around 12,000 BCE marked a turning point in Earth-human relations. This relationship was decisively altered by the Industrial Revolution, which began in Britain in the latter part of the seventeenth century and spread rapidly over Europe and North America in the eighteenth century. This brought the application of power-driven machinery to manufacturing, agriculture, transportation and communications. Hitherto, our ancestors over the earlier millennia were open to receiving what sustenance the Earth would offer through its seasonal bounty. Gradually the human became more proactive by digging and cutting with primitive tools, but the disruptive impact on the planet was minimal until the onslaught of the Industrial Revolution. Since then cutting and digging have been magnified beyond comprehension with mechanised mining and drilling deeper and deeper in order to force access to the secrets of the soil, mineral wealth of rocks, fruits of the forests and hidden treasures of ocean depths.

Through time the natural world became less and less a participant in life's unfolding with vast numbers of people. For many, particularly the more technologically controlled, Earth has to be dominated, subdued and exploited for the sole good of the burgeoning human population. The *Reader's Digest Word Power Dictionary* defines technology as 'the application of scientific knowledge for practical purposes'. Since the beginning humans have used technology; inventiveness is natural. Technology began as a natural extension of the body, for example the arm was extended and empowered by the axe or club, clothing and footwear protected and strengthened the body. Technology became more sophisticated as we see in art, architecture, agriculture, industry, science and so forth. Humans and some animals have evolved an impressive array of tools for living and we are aware of the ease, comfort and possibilities afforded by modern technology. We hold in tension the delicate balance between tools for living and these becoming weapons of aggression, even mass destruction. One of the challenges facing us is to welcome and cherish technology as intrinsic to life and work to maintain its alignment with the basic technologies of the Earth. It is for us to co-operate with and enhance the inner workings of nature, not to redesign these patterns. While technology is a rich asset, it is important that we don't get carried away and, as Einstein had cautioned, create monsters that may eventually enslave us.

A river is often seen as a great metaphor for life; my soul moves deep like the river flowing with the rhythms of nature. Our ancestors were drawn to the vital life force of water, gathering in the flood plains of the world's majestic rivers and waterways. Today technology is being used to straighten and re-direct the course of rivers, for example the Nile (North East Africa), Panama River Basin (South America), and huge dams are being constructed to harness water for rising human populations, for example Tigris and Euphrates (Middle East) and Yangtze (China). The process of artificially changing the course of a river is like locking a person in a straitjacket and throwing away the key. Overuse of concrete and tarmac has the same effect on the body of Earth, the natural stretch and flow is impeded, the soul processes of laughter and yawning are strangled. The American Association for the Advancement of Science (AAAS) in its *Atlas of Population and Environment*, shows how the Earth has been altered by human activity. Humans have regulated the flow of some two-thirds of Earth's rivers and twenty-four per cent of land surface is either under concrete or the plough, this rises to forty per cent if pasture and forestry are included. The atlas tells us that 'we have become a major force of evolution, not just for the new species we breed and genetically engineer but for the thousands of species whose habitats we modify' and while humans are among the most successful species 'our success is showing signs of overreaching itself, of threatening the key resources on which we depend'.

## More Is Never Enough

From the beginning there have been communities, of different ethnic origin, including our early Irish ancestors, who have remained faithful to the partnership bond with planet Earth. These people who touch soul chords within the human psyche hold, I believe, the earth wisdom and guidance that so many of us seek. It is all too evident that the same insanity which drives the devastation of Earth, the exploitation of indigenous peoples, women, of children, of animals, of the educationally and economically disadvantaged, continues to take more sinister twists. There is the onslaught on seeds, on food production, on human and animal bodies, on health and reproduction and on the genetic code and memory sacred to each one of us. I am not opposed to research and development, on the contrary, I marvel at the discoveries of generations, the advances in science, medicine, information technology and communications, psychology, growth and understanding in so many facets of life. The alarm bells ring out when any of these are generated from the point of view and welfare of the human family alone, at whatever cost to the whole community of life. Likewise, when they are primarily economy-driven for the benefit of the affluent to the neglect of the economically-poorer in society, or from the urge to manipulate and control and when patenting becomes the goal.

Current statistics from the UN Food and Agriculture Organisation report that about seventy-five per cent of genetic diversity in agriculture has disappeared during this past century. It is astonishing to think our world relies on four crops, namely maize, rice, wheat and sugar cane, for more than half of its food supply even though there are an estimated 30,000 plant species with edible parts. We Irish, with our history of famine worsened by the dependency on potato monocultures, know first-hand of the limitations of monoculture. Worldwide today there is the added concern of global biopatents – patents on living things, the control and ownership of organisms by large multinational corporations. Vandana Shiva, in her book *Stolen Harvest*,[9] highlights the problem of biopatenting from her native Indian perspective, which has echoes in every society where small farmers are being pushed to extinction as single cropping replaces diversification of crops. 'In Indian culture seeds are sacred', the seed, for the farmer, is not only the source of future food supply 'it is the storage place of culture and history'. Seeds play an important role in religious festivals. The farmer reveres the field 'which, as mother, feeds the millions of life forms that are her children'.

Thirteen multinational companies currently own eighty per cent of patents on genetically modified foods and only five agrochemical companies control almost the entire global genetically modified seed market.[10] In the spirit of Vandana and other voices against corporate monopoly and theft of nature's resources for monetary gain let us wake up to what is happening around us before it is too late. Too late to save and share the seeds of nature and our ancestors in the total life community, too late to preserve living organisms from the stranglehold of biopiracy (the theft through biopatents of diverse species) and too late to be able to enjoy the richness in biodiversity, to save the soul of the soil. May we be heartened in our resolve by the revoking in May 2000 of the notorious Neem tree patent granted to the US multinational W R Grace. The Neem tree has been central to the Indian way of life over millennia for providing clothing, food, shelter, healing and for its spiritual powers. The organised opposition to the patent and resultant victory marks the return of resources from the patent regimes of the North.[11]

## Decision Time

> It is my deep conviction that the only option is a change in the sphere of the spirit, in the sphere of human consciousness. It's not enough to invent new machines, new regulations, and new institutions. We must develop a new understanding of the true purpose of our existence on earth. Only by making such a fundamental shift will we be able to create new models of behaviour and a new set of values for the planet.[12]

Do I really believe that there is hope, that as earthlings we inhabit a beautiful planet, and that we have the ability in partnership with Earth to counter the seemingly wanton devastation being wreaked upon the whole community of life especially in our moment in history? How is our planet unhealthy and who is rendering it so? How and by whom will its vitality be restored? Am I convinced that by not acting I am in fact colluding with the negative and destructive forces subtly at work? Do I care? I may want to do something but will my tiny effort make any difference? As the American anthropologist Margaret Meade said, 'Never doubt that a small group of thoughtful, committed citizens can change the world. Indeed, it is the only thing that ever has.'

## Ecology: An Invitation To Come Home

We live in an age of increasing human domination and exploitation of the Earth's resources, both physical and biological. The challenge facing us is how to reconcile the needs of a growing population with the urgency of creating ways that are environmentally sustainable. Some would argue that there are too many people on planet Earth. Life expectancy is increasing everywhere except in Africa, where AIDS and other infectious diseases are taking a huge toll. World population has more than doubled since 1950 and it is predicted to increase to around 8.9 billion by 2050.[13] Many of the Earth's natural resources are finite not infinite. In order to understand this fact I believe it is important that we acquire some basic knowledge of ecology. How the human species finds its niche in the wider ecology of planet Earth is something we can no longer ignore. The time has come for humankind to cease trying to fit ecology into world market economics and make the courageous transformation of evolving economic systems from an ecological worldview.[14]

The process of tailoring ecology to human created economics is as impossible as trying to squeeze cosmology into religious traditions. The Universe is primary in evolutionary terms, the human derivative. Only when we begin to acknowledge and celebrate this, will we truly come home to who we are as species among species, interdependent and interconnected in the magnificent web of life

> How can we be so poor as to define ourselves as an ego tied in a sack of skin? ...We are the relationships we share, we are that process of relating, we are, whether we like it or not, permeable – physically, emotionally, spiritually, experientially – to our surroundings. I am the bluebirds and nuthatches that nest here each spring, and they too are me. I am no more than the bond between us. I am only so beautiful as the

character of my relationships, only so rich as I enrich those around me, only so alive as I enliven those I greet.[15]

What is ecology? Scientifically it is described as that branch of biology dealing with the relationship of organisms to one another and to their particular physical surroundings. By surroundings or environment (French *'environ'*), is meant the total web of interacting relationships, plants, animals and soil, air, water and climate making up the physical environment with its array of chemical and physical properties. It is not possible to understand why an organism has a particular structure or defined characteristics unless it is studied in its particular environment or habitat. How each organism fits into the pattern of nature forms the basis of the science of ecology. Peter D. Moore, editor of *Ecology, The Web of Life,* describes ecology as 'the art of seeing the whole as well as the pieces; it is the ability to see the wood as well as the trees'.

Ernest Haeckel (1834-1919), a German naturalist, coined the word, 'ecology' in 1866. He invented it from its Greek root *'oikos'*, meaning home or household and combined this with *logos,* also Greek, denoting any kind of study. Ecology is concerned not only with the interaction between living organisms and their environment, but also with the global abundance and distribution of organisms. It is important to understand the wonderful ecological system in which we live. How else can we cherish the amazing gift of life? What other context is there for trying to understand and beginning to solve the problems in our world? The creation of an economic system rooted in ecology would challenge us to come home to our rightful place as species among species in the community of all life, each nourished and energised by the Sun and one another. It is like coming down to Earth from our perch of dominance, acknowledging our roots in holy ground, indeed a conversion from stranger to companion on the journey of life.

## In Nature, Nothing Lives Entirely On Its Own

> We live on a small planet circling a minor star at the edge of an unremarkable galaxy. Life here is sustained by energy from the sun, but is otherwise a 'closed' system – materials are cycled and recycled through earth, air and water by uncounted lives, from microbes to mammals, nothing lost, nothing new.[16]

Ecology as a discipline brings together the discoveries of biology and the observations of natural history. The environment of each individual being is highly complex embracing multiple physical components as well as the influence of all other organisms in the vicinity, whether of the same species or several other species. These may be predator or prey or simply habitat enhancers. The complex web of interrelationships in the natural world poses many questions: why do certain plants and animals live together in distinct communities? Is this a random occurrence? Is it a result of climatic factors? Perhaps, it is a question of dependency, of needing each other for their continued survival? Why are there penguins in the Antarctic but not in the Arctic? This is the domain of ecology and it comprises many levels: *individual*, individual within a *population* and *community*, the interacting of populations of various species in the same place. Some examples of a community may be all the organisms living in an urban garden pond, in a fuchsia hedgerow or in Fota Island National Park in Co. Cork. The process of births, deaths and reproduction, of evolution by natural selection, by which organisms control the composition of a population, is key in ecological understanding.

When the community of living plants and animals is viewed in the context of the physical, geological, chemical and climatic conditions we can see the whole with its component parts or functions. Through photosynthesis, green plants feed on energy from the Sun. These are consumed by grazing animals, which are in turn fed upon by parasites and predators. Dead tissue falls and nourishes the decomposers, both animal and microbe. The minerals in rocks are weathered by the elements thereby releasing life nutrients, which are extracted by plant roots for the nourishment of the whole community of life, only to be released again in an endless cycle.

The study of ecology embraces the total living world. The smallest unit of study is the *niche*, which includes behaviour, diet and the position of a living body in its environment. Then there is the *habitat*, which forms the natural environment of several species. Separate habitats with their flora and fauna make up *ecosystems* and these in turn form the *biomes* that make up the *biosphere* as a whole. Planet Earth is divided into a number of regions that share basically the same type of plant and animal life, called biomes. Different climates create different biomes, some examples include: tropical rainforest, temperate grassland, Mediterranean, desert, mountain, tundra, polar, and coral reef. Some continents feature a variety of biomes – Africa has tropical rainforest, savannah grassland and desert. Ecosystems are complete communities of living beings. All the species are linked through drawing on the same food and energy sources from their surroundings. They are of no specific size and can range from the sycamore tree in the back garden to a coral reef: 'A single pond in Brazil can sustain a greater variety of fish than are found in all of Europe's rivers'.[17] The tropical rainforests of the planet are very rich in biodiversity. They provide numerous niches and several small ecosystems within the main forest ecosystem.

## Deep Ecology

Arne Naess, Norwegian philosopher, developed the idea of 'deep ecology' in the early 1970s. He was acutely aware of the need to move beyond superficial responses to ecological problems to asking questions around the 'why and how' of the way we live and the beliefs and values we espouse. Deep ecology is a more holistic way of looking at life in its multiple relationships and seeing the connections since ecology is not something separate from life, 'out there', as it were, but something we are intimately part of and engaged with in the unfolding of life. Joanna Macy, author and international leader of Deep Ecology Workshops, has this to say:

> Deep ecology serves as the explanatory principle both for the pain we experience on behalf of our planet and its beings, and for the sense of belonging that arises when we stop repressing that pain and let it connect us with our world.[18]

'Systems theory', a way of examining relationship patterns between parts and wholes and organisational principles within these, informs the thinking in deep ecology. The whole is more than the sum of its parts, for example, a person is more than a pile of molecules; he or she is more than a separate individual – family-local community-nation-planet-universe. Deep ecology sees humans both as wholes and part of the eco-system of life on planet Earth. The Gaia Hypothesis, formulated by James Lovelock and Lyn Margulis in the early 1970s, proposed that the various life forms on planet Earth form a related whole, this whole is more than the sum of its parts. Furthermore this whole, *Gaia*, is not reducible purely to studying its parts. The Gaia Hypothesis is central to Deep Ecology.

## Ecofeminism

Francoise d' Eaubonne, a French writer, coined the term 'ecofeminism' in 1974. It represented women's potential for bringing about an ecological revolution to ensure human survival on planet Earth. Such a revolution would entail new gender relations between women and men and between humans and nature. Ecofeminism evolved from the radical feminism of the 1960s and 1970s, which succeeded in dismantling the iron grip of biological determinism that had been used historically to justify men's control over women. Radical feminism exposed the fact that social arrangements held to be natural and timeless had actually been constructed in order to validate male superiority and privilege. Ecofeminism joined with the ecological movement around the time of the first Earth Day in 1970. Since then as a movement, it has been emerging as a major catalyst of ethical, political, social and creative change:

> To care emphatically about the person, the species, and the great family of beings, about the bioregion, the biosphere, and the universe is the framework within which ecofeminists wish to address the issues of our time.[19]

In our time, one wonders who or what the catalyst might be for exposing the relatively recent human construction of institutions and laws that render the human dominant over the natural world.

## Silencing Spring

How one loves to hear the call of the cuckoo bridging spring and summer in our land! What of the skylarks, yellowhammer and warblers struggling to be heard above the din of incessant traffic clogging our villages, towns and cities? The rush to urbanise the landscape, which we are programmed to regard as progress, is extending the human ecological footprint exponentially and rendering entire species homeless or refugees. Will it ever occur to us in our desire, albeit laudable, to promote social housing that we need to expand our inclusion of 'homeless and refugees' to embrace other species? We humans do not exist in isolation, whatever befalls the Earth and its community of life befalls the human.

> We see quite clearly that what happens to the nonhuman happens to the human. What happens to the outer world happens to the inner world. If the outer world is diminished in its grandeur then the emotional, imaginative, intellectual, and spiritual life of the human is diminished or extinguished.[20]

That anyone should be without a home or the basics in life is an indictment of our society and ultimately of each one of us. When I refuse to accept human responsibility for current social and ecological problems and make innocent victims pay, I'm thinking, scheming and behaving as a dysfunctional teenager. We humans are so frenzied and hungry for space, that we build more and more houses, some of them veritable cliff-hangers along our charming and fragile coastline; this is ludicrous. Why should so many of our hedgerows, wetlands and callows (riverside fields that flood in winter and are farmed as meadow and pasture in spring), rapidly disappearing boglands, precious topsoil, areas of wilderness, inspirational wild flower meadows and native woodland, so much of the biodiversity of the natural world, be sacrificed without due consideration of the wider context?

Would it not be more sustainable and genuinely humane to call for a temporary moratorium on habitat uprooting, pending, a critical appraisal of necessary, affordable and maximum-use housing space on our island home, home not only to some 4.5 million human beings, but also to billions of other creatures? Researchers warn us that we are in denial with regard to alcohol and substance abuse, particularly among our teenage population.[21] On the same day national news media reports carried the story of another denial – that Ireland should be included in the decision of European Environment Commissioner Ms Margot Wallstrom, to 'name and shame' for breaches of EU safety rules on waste disposal in landfill sites. This echoes the ongoing denial with regard to the required implementation of Special Protection Areas (SPA) as directed by the EU, particularly the failure to adequately address the effects of cumulative development within SPAs.[22]

If we as a society continue to act out of a radical discontinuity with the natural world and expect our water, soil, vegetation, food and air to become guardians of our harmful chemicals and waste mountains should we be surprised that increasing numbers of our vulnerable young people poison their blood stream, respiratory, nervous and digestive systems through the over-consumption of alcohol and substance abuse?

I recall walking into a shopping mall in Boston a few years ago. I was looking for breakfast cereal. As I ambled down this aisle that seemed more like a town street, I felt overwhelmed by the range of cereals. Suddenly, I had this vision of hectares and hectares of grain caressed by the Sun and swaying gently in the fresh Atlantic breeze. Hedgerows and tall trees, teeming with life, weaved along the edges bordering access roads to the Massachusetts' Turnpike. That once alive granary was now the concrete, the vinyl on which I stood, the steel encaging me. That bountifulness and vitality were stuffed in packages all brightly coloured, doubly wrapped for freshness and draped in brand names and special offers before me on the shelves. I felt momentarily dazed and abandoned my search. This is merely one example of the lure of materialism in our world today. The world of concrete and tarmac, of advertising and virtual reality, manufactured beauty and variety is steadily coaxing us further and further from what is natural, wild and free. Of course we need sufficient to live, as well as variety and choice, but aren't we, particularly in the western world, going a bit too far with our food mountains, bulging landfill sites and rampant consumerism? What is making our plight even more lamentable is that advertisers and corporation executives are laughing all the way to the bank, which is itself a system founded and sustained on debt, our debt.

## Voices of Hope

In 1962, an American naturalist named Rachel Carson, published her fourth book *Silent Spring* in which she questioned the human need to exploit nature. She believed that in the universe, matter is continuous – like a Celtic knot – and that this continuum is the narrative that includes all others. There is only one story, the story of the flaring forth of the universe, in its galactic, solar, earthly and human dimensions. Rachel Carson was advocating a whole new way of thinking about life, about our world as she popularised the idea of ecosystems, a word earlier coined by British plant ecologist A.G. Tansley. In this she was deepening the thoughts of the founder of what we know as the ecological movement, the German naturalist Ernest Haeckel and of the philosopher Heidegger. These in turn were articulating the profound sense of the medieval mystics of the intrinsic oneness of all life, that we are beings among a wonderful community of beings in the family of creation.

**Root Exposure**
When Rachel Carson exposed the radical danger the pesticide DDT was having on plant and animal life and the inherent dangers for all living forms including the human, she aroused a storm of protest. What she was in fact doing was exposing what we now know as corporate America. The commercial world was outraged and some members of the scientific community, threatened in their academic credibility and monetary profits, rushed to assist them in their efforts to trivialise and discredit a factual and indeed seminal work. But the author stood firm and tall: 'When the scientific organisation speaks, whose voice do we hear – that of science? Or of the sustaining industry?'[23] Her message was clear and emphatic: 'It is not possible to add pesticides to water anywhere without threatening the purity of water everywhere'.

### Earth is Alive –Wake Up!

What a wake-up call! Perhaps the time has come for us to
see life as a total interacting system. Planet Earth is a living
organism, alive and sustaining the countless life forms, who
inhabit it. In fact, we could usefully think of the Earth as a
'who' rather than a 'what.' When one thinks of a living
being one thinks of breathing, moving, self-regulating, etc.
The same life-giving and sustaining systems of my own
body and that of many other beings, mirrors those of Earth,
for example, the core, crust and mountain ranges form the
skeleton or frame while the algae, plants and soil, absorbing
and recycling everything, make up the digestive system.
The oceans, rivers and waterways are the blood stream or
the circulatory system, and plants, trees and vegetation of
all kinds form the respiratory system, they are the heart and
lungs of the Earth. A whole host of life forms, from insects,
reptiles, birds, mammals (of which the human is one form),
compose the refinement of sight, hearing, touch, taste and
smell, the sensory organs of planet Earth. In the human the
Earth becomes self-consciously aware.

Our reflective self-consciousness is influenced by our
sensory perceptions, our experience of the tangible, living
world around us. I think of the Earth wake-up call as that of
coming to our senses. Many of us have to rediscover the
sense of smell, touch, taste, sight and hearing in order to re-
inhabit the Earth as species among species in the whole life
community. If we were living on Mars or the Moon our
senses would be influenced by that particular landscape,
more monotonous, largely devoid of life, colour and
fragrance. Planet Earth is suffused with life, music, colour,
fragrance, beauty and fluorescence 'all things speak of God'
(Pawnee). Is there anything more wholesome than the feel

of earth and the taste of organically grown food after shaking off the soil? What could be more melodious than birdsong, particularly the dawn chorus? I love the touch of sunshine, the patter of soft rain on my face and the refreshing evening breeze. Whom among us is not stirred by the sight of the rainbow, the vanishing evening sun chaliced in low clouds over the horizon, the sighting of Venus in the night sky, the laughter of children at play, little lambs enjoying their first taste of life and the serenity of animals grazing? 'I laugh when I hear the fish in the water is thirsty.' (Kabir).

Those who live amid concrete and skyscrapers, in the world of disposables, plastics and computers or programmed in manufactured delights are more likely to forget that our well-being is closely linked to the land. We are the Earth/Universe knowing, acknowledging and celebrating 13 billion years of divine creativity. And we say we are too busy to notice! What are some of the indications that we humans have become estranged from the Earth in her wisdom, flaming beauty and untamed wildness? Some of our attitudes, priorities and behaviours portray a more distant sense, an attitude of superiority and dominance, of disregard, whereby we relate to the planet as an object to be explored, used for our good and greed, controlled, subdued, redesigned and silenced. At best it is regarded by many as a backdrop to life rather than the arena of life.

### Variety is the Spice of Life
Biological diversity refers to the variety of life forms on planet Earth. The rich biodiversity of living things can be divided into five kingdoms: bacteria and blue-green algae, protozoa and algae, fungi, plants and animals. Living things, while

diverse, share much in common, for example, ability to grow and mature, to reproduce and to adapt to changes in their environment. Species are the basic unit of biological classification and the measure of biodiversity. It is estimated that there are about 5 to 10 million living species on Earth[24] or possibly as many as fifty million. It is difficult to give even approximate figures as many species become extinct before they can be categorised. Scientifically, there are only 1.75 million named so far.[25] Global biodiversity is shrinking at an alarming rate particularly because of human pressure, notably deforestation, mechanised agriculture and various industrial practices. It is a fact that major extinctions of species have occurred over eons of time through changing environmental conditions and asteroid or meteorite activity.

In a recent *Irish Times* article, Michael Viney refers to biodiversity as 'the spice of life'. He tells us that conservationists, insisting that biodiversity is basic to Earth's life-support system, warn that the widespread destruction of natural forest and resultant progressive loss of species could destabilise 'the very processes by which the planet services our presence and well-being'.[26] All the food that we consume is supplied by a variety of biological species. Every day, one encounters an amazing diversity of life forms. As well as our food, where we dine, what we wear, grow and even the pets we have come from a wide spectrum of life. We catch colds from viruses and we have both friendly and unfriendly bacteria in our stomachs. Humankind evolved amongst rich diversity, this is in our psyche enabling us to respond in wonder and awe to the delights of the natural world. Thomas Berry cautions that a diminished planet will lead to diminished humans:

> If we have words with which to speak and think and commune, words for the inner experience of the divine, words for the intimacies of life, if we have words for telling stories to our children, words with which we can sing, it is again because of the impressions we have received from the variety of beings about us.[27]

Different habitats have different biodiversity levels. The richest biodiversity on Earth is found in the tropical rainforests with one hectare being home to almost three hundred species of trees. In a four square mile area of Amazon rainforest there are some one and a half thousand species of plants, seven hundred and fifty species of trees, four hundred of birds and twenty-five mammals.[28] Human impact is severely diminishing the world area of rainforest: in the past two hundred years rainforests have dwindled from 1,500 million hectares (size of Europe) to less than 900 million hectares. Coral reefs are rich in marine biodiversity. These are being depleted mainly through global warming as a result of human activity.

In Ireland, the Government's millennium project of planting one million oak trees and the Rural Environment Protection Scheme aimed at limiting damage from farming practices are among a number of positive steps. However, the transition to mechanised farming, the movement to urban areas, the upsurge in building roads and houses is taking its toll on our biodiversity. The widespread removal of hedgerows, trees, grassland and bogland is usurping habitats and causing large-scale dislocation among a growing number of species. BirdWatch Ireland and RSPB Northern Ireland at the beginning of the new millennium compiled a list of endangered birds including: corncrake, curlew, yellowhammer, corn bunting, lapwing, red grouse, chough and barn owl.[29] The dangerous levels of nitrate and other toxins in our waterways are harmful to marine life. Farming practices and industrial waste are being blamed while research into this growing concern continues.

## Trees

Trees are beautiful. This is an understatement. They are indeed a sacred reality enriching both body and soul. I think of trees as the collective memory of creation, the encyclopaedias of the universe. Strolling in the forest is like having a fireside chat with one's ancestors, imbibing ancient wisdom, sharing one's soul longings and speaking one's dreams. One is awakened to growth and abundance, the silent purr of life, the echoes of eternity. Trees remember and respond from an inner secrecy where nothing is forgotten. Our very names are written in this book of life, as we know from the ancient Irish Ogham script. Our mute friends speak a language understood only through being attuned and echoed in a deep sense of belonging:

> My father dreamt forests, he is dead –
> And there are poplar forests in the waste-places
> And on the banks of drains.
> When I look up
> I see my father
> Peering through the branched sky
> > (from 'Poplar Memory' by Patrick
> > Kavanagh).

Trees are home to many species and our early hominid ancestors lived in the trees before standing upright in the African landscape. In the lap of the trees we humans learned the secret of standing upright. They taught us how to sink our roots deep into the heart energies of the universe, to stand tall and face the sunlight with arms outstretched to embrace life in its trillions of guises. From trees we experience the value of silence, of harmony, colour and music, the rhythmic art of letting go into fresher manifestations of vitality and beauty. They grace us aesthetically. They supply our timber, paper and heating resources.

Trees are the lungs of Earth, maintaining the balance of nature as their seasonal changes create a habitat for plants and wild life. They are nature's way of renewing the air that we breathe: they absorb carbon dioxide and give oxygen, which enables all living beings to breathe. Why would anyone want to destroy or fell them unnecessarily? Anyone who has witnessed a loved one dying from respiratory related illnesses is profoundly aware of the need for species that regulate and purify the air we breathe. Conditions in the Irish climate – mild, moist and with good soil and ample water supply - are suited to the rapid growth of trees. The island was once completely forested but now ranks well below the European average. Our forest cover is approximately nine per cent compared with over twenty per cent for the rest of Europe. On a recent visit to the Ecos Centre, Ballymena, Northern Ireland, I found it sobering to learn that it takes about seventeen trees to manufacture one tonne of paper and some 3 billion trees annually to wipe the bottoms of the world!

The tropical rainforests, a relatively small proportion of the Earth's surface, are unique ecosystems as well as vital absorbers of carbon dioxide. The Amazon Rainforest, sometimes described as the 'Lungs of the Planet' is estimated to produce over twenty per cent of the Earth's oxygen. The rainforests are rapidly and often ruthlessly disappearing with almost half of them already destroyed. The destruction of the rainforests is caused by farming practices such as slash-and-burn and shifting cultivation. These are a direct consequence of indigenous people being displaced by multinational companies and large landowners. Another significant cause is tree felling, particularly by logging companies, who with mechanised transport drive deeper and deeper into the rainforests often leaving a trail of destruction behind. It is estimated that one in every two trees is destroyed or damaged by the machinery used to drag the timber away. Other factors include: ranching, mining and burning by arson attack.

Deforestation has devastating effects on the native peoples, on wildlife, on the soil and on climate. Scientists estimate that daily loss of species due to deforestation is somewhere in the region of almost one hundred and forty species of plants, animals and insects. The widespread erosion of topsoil is destroying populations and their livelihoods as well as scarring the Earth and denuding her in obscene ways. Areas rich in rainforests like Indonesia, New Guinea, Borneo, Ecuador and other regions of the Amazon Basin are being decimated as unscrupulous multinational companies exploit these unique environments. The frenzy for oil seems to take precedence over everything else as one hears threats to drill in special areas of conservation such as Alaska. The *Irish Times*, 9 November, 2002 reported on the devastation of Ecuador by US oil companies: 'With at least twenty-five years of oil reserves remaining, neither the Ecuadorian government nor the oil companies are willing to take their heads out of the well. When they do, they will truly see an "empty land"'.

## Precious Water

Long, long ago when Earth was very young, life in the universe was parched and burning with energy. It was the time before hydrogen and oxygen had the opportunity to meet. Mysteriously these two elements were drawn into relationship – the intensity of which continues to flow like a gigantic stream awakening the parched deserts into life. In that moment water was created and so was life. One can only imagine this new substance, liquid, making its way around the planet, oozing through the soil, cascading down the mountains, giving itself to the Sun, the wind and waving in greeting to every revelation of the divine energy. What a gift! Water is the most precious liquid on our planet. It is essential for all living beings. Two-thirds of the Earth's surface is covered with water, but most of this is saltwater and therefore unfit for human or agricultural nourishment. It is amazing to consider, as noted earlier, that a little over two per cent of water on Earth is fresh and of this about two-thirds is locked in glaciers and ice caps. This leaves less than one-hundredth of one per cent drinkable and renewable by precipitation and rainfall each year. Like rocks and air, water is, as we have seen earlier, constantly being recycled within the whole Earth system.

Since the beginning of human presence the Earth's renewable freshwater supply has remained unchanged, but that is changing as the human population increases making the demand for water more acute. The amount of freshwater available to each individual decreases as the population rises. Recent UN statistics indicate that more than 1 billion people in Africa, Asia, and Oceania lack safe drinking water and almost half the current world population (2.8 billion), lack access to minimum sanitation facilities. Globally there is the contrasting scenario between the affluent squandering of water in the West and women and children in the Southern Hemisphere making daily journeys of several miles to fetch water for their families. Precious waterways are becoming political tension points and who knows but in the near future wars will be over water and not oil.

What if we were to regard the water of life on our planet as one gigantic ocean rather than geographical boundaries or political entities named and defined as Mediterranean, Atlantic, Indian, Pacific? This same salt water courses through our bodies and the bodies of all living beings. It is in our tears, our initiation ceremonies and sacramental systems, it is sentiment; it is our life's blood. Are we less sensitive to the evil of pollutants when we regard the oceans as objects, huge, bottomless, distant and all-absorbing of our waste? What discontinuity with life sources causes us to sail off in the dark of the night to dump toxic waste into the lap of our living waters in the hope that it will disappear forever? And that it will not ultimately affect our health and the health of the planet? How would I feel if people were to wantonly offload their waste on my body? Would I consider doing it to any person? Are other beings in the community of life less worthy of due consideration?

## Tasting the Difference

Nowadays, with the rise in industrial agriculture, farmers feed the crop itself, not the soil. Intensive use of pesticides and chemical fertilisers – far in excess of what plants can use – causes serious damage to the natural systems with water, soil and air becoming severely polluted. More and more bumper yields belie the alarming decrease in organic matter and living organisms, which are the soul of soil. The sheer weight of machinery and the overuse of chemicals, many not yet tested for safety, erode the topsoil. This is compounded by the rising trend in animal factories, which produce 1.3 billion tons of manure each year. This manure is full of chemicals, hormones and antibiotics and leaches into the waterways causing widespread pollution and massive fish kills as well as diseases in other species.[30]

In the experience of those reared on organic food before the widespread introduction of chemicals in agriculture there is no mistaking the taste of wholesome food. In more recent times it is so easy to become lured by the cosmetics of supermarkets, 'picked early for freshness' and trebly wrapped for safety! Isn't it strange that we have allowed ourselves to expect fruit and vegetables out of season and fall so easily for the manipulation *en route*, not to mention meat, chicken and eggs from factory farms? And even more that we are willing to purchase as organic, goods that have travelled hundreds and thousands of miles. We now face the challenge of genetically modified organisms (GMOs). Genetic engineering is about inserting genes from one species into another. When genes from different organisms are combined (recombinant DNA technology) the resulting organism is said to be 'genetically engineered' or 'modified'. With regard to GM crops, about ninety per cent of those grown commercially, 'have been engineered to exhibit just two traits – herbicide tolerance and insect resistance'.[31] Among the main foods in this growing GM enterprise are: soybeans, canola (rape), cotton, corn, wheat, rice, barley, sugar beet, tomatoes and sweet potato. In terms of personal choice we should at least be informed of the presence of GMO material in our food products.

Out of Wonder

There is much argument both for and against the genetic engineering of seeds. The principal argument in favour has to do with increasing food production in order to allay world hunger. Viewed systemically this is a contradiction. Who really believes that world hunger and poverty are caused by the lack of food potential on planet Earth? People generally, and small farmers in particular, have saved seeds from year to year and generation to generation. The introduction of the 'terminator' gene[32] in the name of so-called progress is ominous when half the soya planted in tropical countries is from saved seed and some eighty million of India's one hundred million farms depend on saved seeds.[33] Another argument in favour is that food quality will be enhanced and food security increased. This is countered by the potential health impact with regard to the total community of life, for example, cross-pollination and the unknown effects on other organisms, loss of biodiversity, danger to organic cultivation and unknown effects on human health and well-being. On a deeper level there is the violation of the intrinsic value, interiority, of natural organisms. While the technology is advancing it is by no means failure proof. Rachel Carson's words regarding the contamination of water resonate deep within me – how can anyone be sure that modifying seeds anywhere will not ultimately affect seeds everywhere? Moyra Bremner in her book *GE Genetic Engineering and You*, is echoing the sentiments and fears of many:

> This field is dominated by a handful of multinational corporations, most of which originally made their billions in farm chemicals, pharmaceuticals, or both. Some of these new-made gene giants can swallow competitors as easily as a whale scoops up plankton, have budgets larger than New Zealand's and a worldwide web of influence at every level.[34]

## Feeling the Heat

The Sun is the source of all our power. The heat that warms the Earth making it habitable originates from the Sun some 93 million miles distant. It is the greenhouse gases in the atmosphere that regulate the temperature so that plants and animals can flourish. There are some thirty greenhouse gases in the Earth's atmosphere, which have existed naturally for millions of years, these include: carbon dioxide ($CO_2$), water vapour, methane and ozone. In recent years humans have added other gases, for example, chlorofluorocarbons (CFCs) and significantly altered the balance of some existing gases, for example, carbon dioxide and methane. The atmosphere surrounds the Earth like a gaseous envelope and is held by the pull of gravity. The composition of the Earth's atmosphere is as follows: nitrogen seventy-eight per cent, oxygen twenty-one per cent, carbon dioxide 0.03 per cent and other trace gases 0.04 per cent. If the full amount of energy received from the Sun in the form of electromagnetic radiation were to reach the surface of the Earth it would be much too hot for life. Instead about thirty per cent of this energy is reflected back by the atmosphere with forty-seven per cent being absorbed by the atmosphere, the land and oceans. A further twenty-three per cent is used in the water cycle, evaporation and condensation. The remainder is used to drive the winds and ocean currents with a tiny portion used in photosynthesis (the energy locked up in fossil fuels).

Ozone, which is a form of the oxygen we breathe, contains an extra oxygen atom (besides oxygen itself), which makes it poisonous and deadly. It is produced from oxygen in the stratosphere (between 10 and 25 kilometres above the Earth's surface), in a series of photochemical reactions stimulated by sunlight, particularly by ultraviolet radiation.

The action of the Sun is constantly producing and breaking down ozone and maintaining it at a constant level. The ozone layer, so-called because it is more concentrated in the stratosphere, is vital for us in that it absorbs almost all the harmful ultraviolet radiation from the Sun. UV-C is the short-wave radiation that is lethal to all living beings. It is this part that gets through when the ozone layer is damaged.

What causes global warming? We hear so much about it today and also that we are responsible, but many of us are unaware of why it is happening and many more are in denial as to our implication in this harmful process. Energy is everywhere in our universe, it cannot be created or destroyed. So what is the mechanism on planet Earth for regulating the flow of energy, that is removing it at the same rate as it arrives to ensure that the Earth is not to get hotter or colder? This is the role of the atmosphere. The temperature of any radiating body determines the wavelength of radiation. The Sun is extremely hot and gives off radiation of a short wavelength. Some of this is reflected back by the atmosphere but most of the remainder passes through the atmosphere to warm the surface of the Earth. The Earth is much cooler than the Sun so surface heat is radiated back into the atmosphere by long-wave radiation. The greenhouse gases in the atmosphere can absorb the long-wave radiation more easily than the short-wave radiation and as a result the atmosphere is warmed. Therefore the more we contribute to raising the greenhouse gases the warmer the atmosphere.

There is now overwhelming scientific evidence to suggest that the amount of many greenhouse gases in the atmosphere is increasing. British physicist, John Tyndall (1820-1823) discovered that carbon dioxide is transparent to light but blocks heat. $CO_2$ is the most common greenhouse gas and is responsible for almost half of the extra warming that is taking place, but other gases, for example, CFCs are thousands of times more effective.[35] Duncan Stewart, in *The State We're In*, tells us that Ireland has one of the highest emissions of greenhouse gases in Europe per capita with a 32.1 per cent increase between 1990 and 2000. As one among 180 countries signing the Rio Agreement (1992) and Kyoto Protocol (1997), Ireland has committed to reducing emissions to thirteen per cent above the 1990 levels by 2012. One would be forgiven for being sceptical about the government's seriousness with regard to environmental priorities in light of recent budgets and particularly with further motorway plans for this relatively small and beautiful land. There is no doubt that we require good roads, but criss-crossing this island with motorways is highly questionable.

**Upsetting the Balance**
Climate change has already arrived. We don't have to wait for it, but how certain can we be that, as alleged, humans are to blame for it? In 1988 the United Nations formed a body of scientists, economists and policy makers – The Intergovernmental Panel on Climate Change – to inform governments of the likely causes and consequences of climate change. Their brief also included searching for solutions to this global problem. Twelve years on they published their *Third Assessment Report* with some startling news. Not only was global warming occurring but that it is predominantly human-made and is increasing faster than previously thought.[36] Temperatures, especially night-time averages, are rising, the planet's snow cover is decreasing, polar ice caps are melting and glaciers in non-polar regions are also retreating; all indicative of rapid change. It is a fact that many different

factors contribute to global warming, for example, erupting volcanoes and sunspot activity, but evidence is now stronger than ever before that human activities have contributed enormously over the past fifty years. The main culprit appears to be the dramatic rise in $CO_2$, up 31 per cent since 1750. According to the IPCC this rise is unprecedented in the past 20,000 years. Other gases in the culprit category include methane and CFCs.

The rise in $CO_2$ emissions has accelerated since the Industrial Revolution with the increase in the burning of fossil fuels (coal, oil, natural gas) thereby releasing the carbon locked up in them into the atmosphere as $CO_2$. Sea algae and plants absorb $CO_2$ as they grow but they are unable to absorb it at the accelerated rate at which it is now entering the atmosphere. It is estimated that human activities add an extra 5 billion tonnes of $CO_2$ to the atmosphere each year so that our atmosphere now contains more $CO_2$ than there has been since humankind evolved. The burning of fossil fuels, which are the remains of dead plants and animals containing carbon absorbed millions of years ago, has increased global warming by about 40 per cent. Cars, vans, lorries, buses, trains and especially aeroplanes add millions of tons of $CO_2$ yearly.

In Asia, scientists have identified the 'Asian Brown Haze', a three-kilometre deep blanket of ash, acids, chemical droplets and a host of other particles stretching across southern Asia. There are global implications here since this sort of cloud of sooty pollution can travel around the globe in a matter of weeks. The executive director of the United Nations Environment Programme (UNEP), at a recent conference in London (August 2002), points to forest fires, the burning of agricultural wastes, fossil fuels from vehicles and power stations together with emissions from millions of inefficient cookers as the likely cause of such pollution. Research showed that the amount of solar energy reaching the Earth's surface is reduced by ten to fifteen per cent.

## Methane Menace

Methane gas is about twenty times more effective as a greenhouse gas than $CO_2$ and it is increasing about four times faster than $CO_2$. What is methane gas? It is the gas produced when bacteria break down organic matter without the presence of oxygen. Areas such as swamps, waste dumps, paddy fields and the guts of cattle and termites are home to millions of these bacteria. These sources have greatly increased through human activity. Domestic cattle produce more methane than animals of the wild. In Ireland, for example, there are twice as many cattle as people with nine out of every ten destined for world markets. The production of methane gas by the animals themselves 'is the single largest factor contributing to Ireland's greenhouse gas emissions, accounting for one-third'.[37] One can only imagine the contribution in countries like the United States where nearly seventy per cent of grain production is fed to livestock mainly to supply burger outlets. Paddy fields (rice being one of the four crops supplying over half of world food), covering some 1.5 million square kilometres are probably the single largest source of methane. With our mounting waste and bulging landfill sites, methane gas is released into the atmosphere in rising quantities.

### Waste-Away

Over the centuries, nature's recyclers – fungi, bacteria, worms – have evolved a strategy to deal with organic waste. With the introduction of plastics and a growing variety of human-made materials, which our natural recyclers cannot adapt to, the amount of rubbish destined to litter the planet for generations to come is enormous.

Our waste falls into two main categories, namely biodegradable and non-biodegradable. The former is organic matter coming originally from living things and can therefore be broken down given the right conditions. The latter however, cannot be broken down; some of it will disintegrate over time but most of it will remain unaltered. We are slowly waking up to the fact that our waste crisis will not go away. Duncan Stewart reminds us that in Ireland we commit a staggering ninety-seven per cent of our waste to landfill, one third of which is organic waste, which could be composted. Friends of the Earth have calculated that in the United Kingdom annually some twenty million tonnes of rubbish are thrown from our homes. As governments, under increasing public pressure, struggle with issues of landfill, incineration and recycling facilities, each one of us has our part to play. The primary goal is reduction followed by recycling, repairing and reusing and these demand choices and decisions that are often counter-cultural. The recent increase in recycling facilities is commendable and judging by the response of individuals and neighbourhoods they will continue to expand. The promotion of composting of organic waste at local council level is encouraging. We like to be creative, what better way than assisting in the growth of soil?

Only when the last tree has died and the last river poisoned and the last fish been caught will we realise that we cannot *eat money*. (Cree Indian Saying).

I like to image our journey in reconnecting more deeply with the natural world as a process from *dependency* through *independency* to *interdependency*. In the beginning there was an obvious reliance on the Earth as provider (dependence); gradually humans, particularly in the western world, began to assume control of production (independence), while many today realise the wisdom in recognising and honouring our radical interconnectedness and interdependence as species among species in the intricate web of life (interdependence). Thomas Berry sees the immediate imperative before us as 'that the human community and the natural world will go into the future as a single sacred community or we will both perish on the way'.[38]

## Notes

1. A 'bioregion' refers to an area with 'leaky boundaries', which is characterised by a variety of natural features – flora, fauna, soil, climate, geology and geography, history, archaeology, folklore, culture, agriculture and industry.
2. *The Universe Story* Brian Swimme & Thomas Berry, 180-81, (HarperSanFrancisco, 1992).
3. *No City Limits* article by John Reader in the *Guardian* September 11 2004.
4. The Justice Policy Institute quoted in *Resurgence* 14 May/June 2001.
5. *Why Ecovillages?* Helena Norberg-Hodge, 38, *The Ecologist* Vol 32 No 1, February 2002. Recommended reading: *And We Are Doing It, Building an Ecovillage Future* by J.T. Ross Jackson (Robert D. Reed Publishers, San Francisco, 2000)

6.  *Canticle to the Cosmos* Brian Swimme Tape 12 'A New Prosperity' (Sounds True Audio, Boulder CO, 1990).
7.  *All About Compost* by Pauline Pears, 26, (Search Press, London, 1999).
8.  *Donegal for All Seasons* by Liz Sheppard, 164, (Donegal Democrat Ltd, Ballyshannon, Ireland, 1992).
9.  *Stolen Harvest* by Vandana Shiva (South End Press, Cambridge, MA, 2000).
10. *Voice of Irish Concern for the Environment* (Dublin, Ireland, 2001).
11. *The Ecologist*, 8, June 2000.
12. Vaclav Havel, 'Introductory Essay' in *Creating a World that Works for All* by Sharif Abdullah, viii, (Berrett-Koehler , San Francisco, 1999).
13. State of the World 2004 , (The Worldwatch Institute USA, 2004).
14. For fuller analysis see *The Great Work* by Thomas Berry (Bell Tower, New York, 1999) *Eco-Economy: Building an Economy for the Earth* by Lester Brown (W.W. Norton & Company, 2001).
15. *A Language Older Than Words* by Derrick Jensen, 126-127, (Context Books, New York, 2000).
16. *The Gaia Peace Atlas* General Editor Dr Frank Barnaby 10, (Introduction Pan Books, London) 1988).
17. *Herbal Secrets of the Rainforest* by Leslie Taylor (Prima Publishing, Inc., USA, 1998).
18. *Despair and Personal Power in the Nuclear Age* Joanna Macy (New Society Publishers, 1983).
19. 'Ecofeminism: Our Roots and Flowering' by Charlene Spretnak in *Reweaving The World*, eds., Irene Diamond and Gloria F. Orenstein (Sierra Club Books, San Francisco, 1990).
20. *The Great Work* by Thomas Berry, 200, (Bell Tower Publishers, New York, 1999).
21. RTÉ news report 1 October 2002
22. For a comprehensive account of this topic see 'Ireland Taken to Task' by Christine Croton in *Wings, The Quarterly Magazine of BirdWatch Ireland* , 8-9, Number 24, Spring 2002.
23. John Burnside 'Reluctant Crusader' the *Guardian Saturday Review* May 18, 2002.
24. *Cassell's Atlas of Evolution*, 344, (Andromeda Oxford Ltd., 2001).

25. *World Atlas of Biodiversity* Brian Groombridge & Martin D. Jenkins, 16, (University of California Press, Berkeley, Los Angeles, 2002 ).
26. The *Irish Times Weekend*, 7, 27 July 2002.
27. *The Dream of the Earth* Thomas Berry, 11, (Sierra Club Books, San Francisco, 1988 ).
28. *Disappearing Forests*, 5, (Friends of the Earth Trust, London, September 1998).
29. Published in *Wings* Summer 2000.
30. For comprehensive analysis of industrial agriculture, the myths exposed see: *The Ecologist*, 19-24, November 2002.
31. *The Ecologist* July/August 2003, 32 Chelsea Wharf, London UK.
32. The terminator seed, while looking and growing like normal seeds, is technologically programmed to render its own offspring sterile.
33. *Genetic Engineering And You* by Moyra Bremner, 268-9 , (HarperCollins, 1999).
34. Ibid., 13-14
35. Information source: ENFO Publications, Fact Sheets 16 and 25 (Dublin, Ireland).
36. IPCC: Summary for Policymakers, Third Assessment Report, March 2001.
37. *Telling it like it is – Too Many Cows*, 64, (Earth Summit Ireland, 2002).
38. 'The Primordial Imperative' by Thomas Berry in *EarthEthics* Vol.3, No.2 (Center for Respect of Life and Environment, Washington, DC, 1992).

# OUT OF RESPECT

## All is One

Our contemporary world is awakening once again
to the reality and wonder of the earth
Thomas Berry

Bridget Dirrane was born in 1894 on the island of Inishmore,
one of the Aran Islands, which lie off the west coast of
Galway in Ireland. She had the notoriety of being one of
Ireland's two oldest women before she passed away at the age
of one hundred and nine at the end of 2003. Bridget lived life
to the full. She was a nurse, mechanic and freedom fighter
and lived for almost forty years in Boston, USA before
returning to her beloved Inishmore when she was seventy-
two. Shortly before her death last year Bridget wrote: 'You
may ask what I will leave behind me when I go for good? It
won't be riches. What I will leave is the sunshine to the
flowers, honey to the bees, the moon alone in the heavens for
all those in love and my beloved Aran Islands to the seas.'[1] I
mention this great woman as a model for our time. What
insight, what wisdom and respect for the community of life
her dying thoughts convey.

In the earlier part of this book we have followed the evolving story of the Universe in its various forms, rhythms, voices and movements. The central message of the story of life, our story, is that all is one. Our earliest ancestors were acutely aware of this oneness. And, as we have seen, there has been a gradual movement, accelerated in recent centuries, away from intimacy with the natural world. How might we regain some of the composure that comes from a more mutually enhancing relationship between the natural and human world? I believe we need a new vision for our time, a fresh perception of reality, a paradigm shift. This is a worldview or set of assumptions that tells us why things are as they are.

The new story of the Universe, outlined in the epic of evolution over 13 billion years in the preceding chapters, offers a new transforming context for our lives, our hopes and dreams. This vision of the oneness of all life, one living system, one enchanting story for all, is born out of the radical engagement between human spirituality and science. Herein the physical and spiritual development of the evolving universe is synthesised for the first time. This vision of hope is informed by various strands of wisdom: the scientific discoveries through our telescopes and microscopes, especially during the past four hundred years; the earth wisdom of indigenous peoples throughout our world; the collective feminine wisdom; the wisdom of our classical civilisations and religious traditions, the astuteness of artists, poets and writers and the transforming wisdom garnered through our encounters with the whole community of life.

'There is one thing stronger than all the armies of the world and that is an idea whose time has come' (Victor Hugo). In looking to the future with hope, my main thesis will centre on the intrinsic unity of all life and why it is imperative that we reconnect more deeply with the natural world and find our rightful place within it. It is a fact that the human system is part of the greater planetary system, which is part of the galactic system and ultimately of the universe system. Therefore, the articulation of a way forward that is sustaining of life in all its forms must arise out of the consciousness of the total community of life rather than the human only. We have seen in the previous chapter how human creativity and genius, while contributing so richly in many ways, has led and continues to lead to a fundamental estrangement between the human and natural world. We are being called to reconnect more deeply with our ancestral sense of being part *of* the Earth rather than apart *from* the Earth. We are indeed *of* the Earth, not *on* planet Earth.

The shift then is from acknowledging the human alone as central to acknowledging all of creation (including the human) as central and allowing this to shape our attitudes, values, priorities and actions. This will mean a whole new way of being in the world, influencing our thinking, policy setting and decision-making. It is about a way of living rather than an issue added on to an existing list of pressing issues. Where I actually stand will determine how I see reality – apart *from* or part *of* the entire community of the universe. A vivid and living sense of groundedness in the totality of life is the immortal legacy of people like Bridget Dirrane. Who else could acknowledge that the Aran Islands belong to the seas? Perhaps our generation, more than any other, is being challenged to live with the respect that enables us to see each life form as dignified in its own right and valued in its uniqueness, rather than in its usefulness to the human community.

## A New Language

People and nations in the western world generally think of themselves as democratic. Many wars are fought, countless lives are lost among all species and untold destruction of the natural world occurs in the name of democracy. What is democracy? It is about having a voice in the exercise of power, the power that governs our lives. Historically, humans have regarded their societies as democratic even when women and slaves have been excluded from public debate and decision-making processes. Is democracy operative when the mentally, physically, socially or materially challenged are ignored? How different might today's society be if it had grown from the earlier matrilineal model, rather than from the patriarchal societies of Greece & Rome? Can we really hold that we are living democratically today when our lives are subtly (even blatantly) controlled and our actions dictated by corporations and monetary institutions? Even sport has become the vehicle for compulsive advertising and corporate propaganda.

Where is democracy when the air we breathe is polluted with human-made toxins and chemicals, the water we need for life fouled and the soul of soil sullied with pesticides? Powerful examples are everywhere and we are allowing ourselves to become more and more disempowered as people with ideas and plans for a more wholesome quality of life for all. Where is the democratic voice as genetically modified crops invade huge swathes of the planet and make a mockery of personal choice? Can democracy be alive and well when the natural capital of our planet is being ruthlessly squandered by the few controlling the dollar, euro, sterling or yen? How democratic is it to overturn a decision to introduce carbon tax so as not to rock the boat? The insight of Rachel Carson continues to haunt us. Whose voice controls? How might we begin to confront the 'big guys'? Radical democracy, I believe, has to include not only the human voice, but also the other than human. Who is going to be a voice for the voiceless in the community of life, the ones who don't count when constitutions are being written, policies being formulated, decisions being made and monies allocated? We need to expand our ideas of inclusiveness beyond gender, race, creed and colour to species as well. Anything less will keep us undemocratic. We are engaging in a radical democracy and part of that radical shift is in language. The word democracy is centred on the human (Greek: *'demos'*, 'the people', and *'kratia'*, 'power / rule'); we must live ourselves into a new way of thinking, naming and including. A radical shift in worldview challenges us to evolve a language more inclusive of all. Some suggest that we move beyond the limits of democracy to biocracy,[2] whereby the community of all creation is acknowledged, reverenced and respected.

## A Parable of Good Work

Once upon a time, so the story goes, there was a small village at the edge of a river. The people there were good and life in the village was good. One day a villager noticed a baby floating down the river, he jumped in and swam out to save the baby from drowning. The next day he noticed two babies in the river. He called for help and both babies were rescued. And the following day four babies were caught in the turbulent current. And then there were eight, then more and still more. The villagers quickly organised themselves, setting up watchtowers and training teams of swimmers who could resist the swift waters and rescue the babies. Rescue squads were soon working twenty-four hours a day and each day the number of helpless babies floating down the river increased. While all the babies could not be saved, the villagers felt they were doing well to save as many as possible, indeed the village continued on that basis.

One day, however, someone raised the question: 'But where are all these babies coming from? Who is throwing them into the river? Why? Let's organise a team to go upstream and see who's doing it.' The elders countered with apparent logic: 'And if we go upstream who will operate the rescue operations? We need every concerned person here.' 'But don't you see?' cried a lone voice, 'If we find out who's throwing them in, we can stop the problem and no babies will drown. By going upstream we can eliminate the problem.' 'No, it is too risky!' And so the number of babies in the river increased daily. The number of those saved increased, but the number of those who drowned increased even more. (Author Unknown)

I'm sure this parable touches chords deep within us. Will it remain a case of déjà vu? I'm convinced that the time has come for us to awaken from our isolation and direct our primary energies, expertise and resources into preventative action. From the perspective of the community of life we need to become more and more involved in systemic change, transforming underlying structures that are no longer enhancing of life, equality and freedom for all species. We know that remedial care will always be with us, but as the old adage cautions: 'prevention is better than cure'. There will always be the voices telling us that it is 'too risky', or that people always matter more than other beings, or that some people matter more than others, and so it continues.

## Bone-sense

Deep within our ecological sinews, muscles and bones we know the reality. The writing is on the wall. If we don't learn to respect the Earth and live 'more lightly', then there won't be an Earth worth living in. 'Is the human a viable species on an endangered planet?' (Thomas Berry). We live in the best and the worst of times. We inhabit a beautiful planet. We live amid abundance of natural vitality and richness. There is so much good in our world, technological advances have brought widespread prosperity and, as the above parable highlights, there is no scarcity of goodwill and generosity among the vast majority of people: 'We possess infinite altruism' (Dalai Lama). We have never before experienced such global proportions of communications or such extraordinary discoveries in technology, science, medicine, psychology and psychiatry. Why then is there such inequality, oppression, exploitation, hunger, disease and violence? It seems to me that we are engaged in a Sisyphean struggle.[3] What is being created on the one hand is being thwarted on the other, like the heroic efforts of the villagers in the parable. The more they toiled to save the drowning babies the more they were overwhelmed by the sheer magnitude of the problem. Our present day victims of oppression – whether oppressed because of their gender, race, creed, class, sexual orientation, mental or physical abilities, or species – are like the drowning babies, and the few voices for systemic change are likewise unheeded by the 'elders' of the corporate world, of consumerism, selective prosperity, progress and the status quo at any cost.

Respect

## All is One

What underlying assumptions or perceptions of reality do we need to change in order to engage in the transforming vision of life as one total system? I see the primary conversion as that from the human *and* the rest of creation to the human *within* the community of all life. All of created reality is one; interconnected at the deepest level and interdependent. It is a matter of broadening the context, of seeing with new eyes and feeling with awakened hearts the reality of the oneness of all life forms. Our earliest ancestors knew this; indigenous peoples live in this consciousness and many of us yearn for it to become a reality in our lives knowing that we ignore it at our peril.

Ervin Laszlo, author of *Introduction to Systems Philosophy*,[4] states that if we are to understand our place in the totality of life and what we are faced with in the social and natural world, evolving systems is imperative. The systems view always treats systems as integrated wholes, more than the sum of their parts, never as mechanistic aggregates of parts. According to Laszlo, the systems view of nature and man is clearly non-anthropocentric, but it is not non-humanistic for all that. It allows us to understand that the human is one species of system in the larger system of nature and at the same time that all systems, which are sub-systems of the Earth/Universe system, have value and intrinsic worth. We may not be the centre of the Universe or the pinnacle of creation but we do embody a particular cosmic process. We have the remarkable gift of self-reflection.

Hildegarde of Bingen, Mechtild of Magdeburg, Meister Eckhart, Julian of Norwich, St Francis and St Clare of Assisi, to mention but a few, shared a profound sense of the unity of creation. All creatures are kin, born out of the creative energy emerging from the Godhead. 'Holy persons draw to themselves all that is earthly... The earth is at the same time mother. She is mother of all that is natural, mother of all that is human. She is the mother of all, for contained in her are the seeds of all.' (Hildegarde of Bingen). The natural world is not simply a place of wilderness and chaos to be avoided or tamed and domesticated by humans but a subject evoking awe, wonder, praise and thanksgiving. 'The fullness of joy is to behold God in everything' (Julian of Norwich).

Teilhard de Chardin was acutely aware of the oneness of all life. He identified the human as a dimension of the universe from the beginning; all of life was potentially present in the original fireball *c* 13 billion years ago. In 1930 he wrote *Building The Earth*, which was the first form of his *The Phenomenon of Man*, in which he asserts that 'the only truly natural and real human unity is the Spirit of The Earth'.[5] He was committed to the evolutionary process, the acceptance of which in the light of faith was generally problematic for Christians at that time. He told the story of the evolving universe in an integral manner. For him the story of the birth of the galaxies, of emergent Earth within the Solar System, of the profusion of life forms and of human arrival was one story, a unity. The divine is intrinsic to creation and matter has a psychic as well as a physical dimension, the universe has been endowed with this psychic consciousness from the beginning:

> Without the slightest doubt there is something through which material and spiritual energy hold together and are complementary. In the last analysis, somehow or other, there must be a single energy operating in the world. And the first idea that occurs to us is that the

'soul' must be as it were a focal point of transformation at which, from all points of nature, the forces of bodies converge, to become interiorised and sublimated in beauty and truth.[6]

## The Real Cost

In order to illustrate how crucial it is that we begin to shift from the human only to the human within the entire community of life, I want to use the example of the so-called Third World Debt. I refer to this both in its literal and symbolic sense. To my mind the idea of 'debtor' is a powerful metaphor for our time. I view it as a bridge between what is and what can be in our world if only we are alert to the real cost in terms of the total community of life. Lest we forget, in evolutionary terms the Earth is primary – a cell of the universe – the human derivative – a cell of the Earth.

In 1973 members of the Organisation of Petroleum Exporting Countries (OPEC), quadrupled the price of oil and invested their excess money in commercial banks. The banks, seeking investments for their new funds, made loans to developing countries. This was often carried out without evaluation or monitoring, which inevitably resulted in money borrowed and spent without benefiting the materially deprived and most vulnerable people. In 1979 oil prices increased again and this, combined with the adoption of extremely tight monetary policies to reduce inflation by financially better off nations, resulted in a drastic decline in exports from developing countries. This in turn led to widespread poverty, hunger and hardship for millions of people. Ever since then, the materially poorer nations have been forced to sell off their basic living resources – financial, social and environmental – to allay merely the interest on the international loans. It is all too obvious that a growing number of these so-called debtor nations will never be able to do anymore than at present, Mexico has declared thus since 1982.[7] Many national and international organisations and groups made heroic efforts to secure a cancellation of all these outstanding 'debts' before the turn of the millennium. At best, this met with a gesture of good will with minimal reduction ensuring the ongoing oppression of people and planet.

When this issue of debt is viewed from a human centred perspective it seems clear that money has been borrowed and therefore must be paid back with interest. However, if one were to take the wider cosmic view, in which the total community of life is considered, my question would be: 'Who is the real debtor?' In terms of the exploitation and plundering of the rich natural resources of these less economically developed countries and the manipulation and oppression of their populations in multinational workplaces, could the economically wealthier countries ever pay off their debts? These debts include ecological, economical, psychological, educational, health and rightful access to legitimate information.

Deeper questions need to be considered and accountability demanded. The interests of the many – that is, all species – must balance the interests of the few in our interconnected and interdependent community of life. For example, to pay Tiger Woods for a single day's endorsement, Nike spends the equivalent of the daily wages of 14,000 Thailand Nike sub-contract workers.[8] Simon Retallack, in his article 'Why Are We Failing The Planet?', illustrates the environmental impact of economic globalisation when he cites an advert places in *Fortune* magazine by the Philippine Government:

> To attract companies like yours – we have felled mountains, razed jungles, filled swamps, moved rivers, relocated towns – to make it easier for you and your business to do business here.[9]

### Fount of Wisdom
Where shall we look for guidance in order to regain our composure as cosmic beings? Perhaps, it is time for us to acknowledge that our cultural traditions are no longer adequate. We need to peel back the layers and delve into the deep mysteries of our existence. We may call it an expansion of consciousness as we get in touch with our genetic coding beyond our cultural coding and hence to the Earth itself, the ground of our being. And ultimately to the Universe, the carrier of meaning, value and the profound mystery of our existence within itself: 'We have no existence except within the earth and within the universe.'[10]

### Universal Principles
The story of the Universe is a lively account of the energies of life. If one were to listen to the echoes of creativity and chaos deep within the heart of the cosmos as our Universe utters its own story, what a revelation – spontaneity, unpredictability, turbulence, complexity, inventiveness – would become manifest. Each breakthrough moment in the awesome mystery of evolution fascinates us as much by what might have been as by what actually emerged. The image of a forest speaks to me of this profundity. A forest is much more than a sheltering array of trees. It is a veritable symphony

responding to the rhythms of the elements and vibrating with life that emerges from deep under the forest floor skyward beyond the leafy canopies. The chimes of life mingling with the dance of insects, birds, animals, grass, trees, plants and flowers and the quieter chorus of the recyclers – bacteria, fungi and worms – create melodies of soul. A walk among the trees in mellifluous splendour calls one to attentiveness, a sense of abandonment to mystery. Forests are enchanting places, overwhelming too. So much is visible and so much invisible like the story of life, the mystery of the universe:

A magnolia's full throated flowers
open for arias in spring,
but trees in winter show you
their true shape. You belong to something
magnificent that begins in darkness
below the ground. It branches out
but keeps the center aligned,
stands through the seasons and trusts
its small seeds to the wind. By the time
a seed becomes a tree, it can teach you
to free your own dry leaves to dance.[11]

**Unity in Diversity**
The Universe awakens into being as spontaneities of energy governed by the internal orderings or guiding principles of differentiation (diversity), subjectivity (interiority) and interconnectedness. At all levels of reality these three basic laws identify the nature of the Universe, the inherent values and the particular direction in which it is proceeding. They are like the backbone or bloodstream of the Universe shaping reality and guiding the course of life. Have you ever seen two

identical beings among humans, trees, birds or stars? It may appear as if the baby ducks on the pond are identical or the twin girls across the street or surely the peas in the pod fresh from the earth? The truth is that nothing in the universe repeats and the more intimately we get to know something the clearer it manifests its own identity. This is true of all beings in the universe – atoms, stars, galaxies, nebulae, planets, bacteria, insects, plants, animals and humans.

To be is to be differentiated. Without difference there is no creation or expansion. Through the process of differentiation the universe remains one or whole yet stays open to transformation. Diversity is so profuse that while there are particular groupings and bondings, these are themselves differentiated, for example, among and between species: elm and oak, wren and robin, woman and man, the lamb and lion or the butterfly and badger. Differentiation is the process through which the universe sustains life. Male and female must be differentiated for reproduction. On the human level we know that a Maori cannot be a Celt or an Inca an Inuit and so forth. Language and words must be differentiated for meaning. In music, notes are differentiated to harmonise in melody. Likewise with the artist's strokes, the dancer's steps and poet's words; all combine to proclaim their essence.

The direction of the Universe is into differentiation. The raging energy of the original fireball fragmented into galaxies, stars, planets and a living solar system. From stardust all of life as we know it evolved. The Universe could have been a homogenous smudge but the mystery of differentiation changed all that forever. In the beginning, the universe was, for a very short time, pure hydrogen, but it rapidly changed into other elements. When two differentiated things come together the result is further creativity and diversity. A good example of this is the creation of water. Hydrogen, a light colourless, odourless gas combined with oxygen, another colourless, odourless, tasteless gaseous element, to form water. In this creative endeavour, hydrogen remained hydrogen and oxygen remained oxygen but their fusion of energies produced water. What a miracle! Is there an encouraging lesson here for us in our human dreams and enterprises? Our latent energy and creativity reach out in expectancy, awaiting the spark to fan them into living flames for life and abundance. We tend to believe that this reciprocity can come only from other human beings. What untapped potentialities, opportunities and wisdom might there be in our greater interaction with planet Earth and the whole community of life?

One of the contributions of modern science is that it shows us that our universe continues to differentiate itself through time. Things never repeat, the Universe is not cyclical in nature; it is forever in the process of becoming. I am forever in process of becoming, of giving birth to myself, so too is the horse, the rose and the turtle. We are forever shedding our skin; life renewing itself is intrinsic to existence. Do I look or think exactly as I did this time last year? How different shall I be five years hence? It can be both hilarious and sobering to look at earlier photographs of ourselves. It is in essence the same old me but the passing years shift the contours. This amazing lack of repetition lies at the heart of the story of the Universe. In the early life of the universe different minerals came together to form the Earth's crust, which gradually dissolved into soil, vegetation and oceans, which further differentiated into plankton, fish, whales, insects, birds, animals and us. We in the total community of life inhabit a differentiated planet. Each of earth's regions is different and gives life to differing species. The tundra is not rainforest nor is the arctic savannah. Human history with its diverse civilisations, new forms of social and religious institutions and cultural diversity continues the differentiation process that began almost fourteen billion years ago. Everything was potentially there in the original fireball. I am the universe and the universe is me; similarly for the dandelion, the spider or the fox.

## Delight in Difference

The real function of the human is to delight in and celebrate difference. However, we are the only species who seem to have difficulty with diversity, often treating it as a problem to be solved rather than delighting in it as a principle of the universe and of life as a whole. Our problem is that we have come to believe the divine is solely in our image thereby disallowing any differentiation from ourselves. All that God creates is in God's image; each being is distinct but not separate. God cannot create another deity nor communicate God's self totally to any single being; God 'creates this array of beings so that the perfection lacking in one would be supplied by the other, and the total universe of things would manifest and participate in the divine more than any single being'.[12] In virtue of the quality of differentiation as a core value of the universe our first ethical obligation is to acknowledge and reverence the natural world in its uniqueness, beauty, wildness, variety and ferocious energy. Each being deserves to be respected, nurtured and protected in order to fulfil its particular role in the order of creation.

Contemplating the miracle of diversity stirs us to reverence and respect for each being as revelatory of the divine and deserving of mutual nurturing, protection and space to realise its proper mode of presence in the order of things. If we believe in differentiation as a universal principle, can there be hierarchies in terms of gender, ethnicity, sexual orientation, class, creed or species? Can we continue to map our planet earth in terms of nations, states, colonies instead of exploring more 'community of life' models such as bioregions where rocks, soil, climate, flora and fauna are accorded their unique voice alongside the human? How might we celebrate differentiation as an influential value in life? Gradually more people are looking to graced moments in the sacredness of life in the universe as opportunities to celebrate our oneness, our membership of the primary community of all creation. Such occasions include the solstice and equinox in the calendar year highlighting the journey of the Sun, which is the source of all life on planet Earth. Others might be delighting in and celebrating the first shoots of spring like snowdrops, fresh buds on trees, the coming of the rains, the faltering voices of the newborn in all species or the turning of the first sod of earth for planting. If we were to live by differentiation would there be any need for intensive military presence in particular areas as experienced in our world today? What would differentiation look like among the world's religions?

## Interiority – Melodies of Soul

The second tendency of the universe is towards self-organisation within and self-expression without. Every single being has its interiority or subjectivity. Every atom, star, tree, flower, human, insect, animal has its own essence and truth, its own inner authority and peculiar mode of self-manifestation to the world. Each is unique and irreplaceable.

Each is subject, a cell of the earth, a living organism. As members of the primary community – the total community of life in the universe – each is a centre of spontaneity and feeling, endowed with their own specific quality of presence, of self expression, of revealing their inner core, music, colour, contours, seeds, contradictions and possibilities. Each one absorbs the Sun's light and shines forth with their own light, for example, the daisy beams as the 'day's eye', the lake displays lake-light, the rock manifests rock-light and each one of us radiates our own human filtered light. Our common roots are firmly in the divine, the creative energy of the Godhead from which all came to be and whose voice can be heard in the rhythms and rumblings of our expanding universe.

We are called to obedience, a particular mode of listening, of attuning ourselves to the heartbeat of the Universe pulsating in every life form. Human subjectivity holds us open to the magnificence and pain of the Universe. In our present environmental crisis it is obvious that the human community is operating out of an isolated mindset. If we were to consider each being as subject with inner essence and truth would we continue to pollute, destroy and ravage the earth? By beginning to acknowledge and reverence each as subject we will begin to turn the tide of consumerism and waste. I believe that I will be able to recognise the other as subject with interiority to the extent that I value my own interiority and celebrate it. Eckhart Tolle, in his book *The Power of Now*, reminds us that by our failure to live in the present moment we are out of touch with our own inner depths thus creating unhappiness which pollutes not only ourselves but all around us: 'If humans clear inner pollution, then they will also cease to create outer pollution'.[13] The mystery and magic of life in so many and varied forms speak of the ingenuity and hunger of the universe to come alive. Let us take note and proclaim this awesomeness in the way that we live and love. In his book *The Dream of the Earth*, Thomas Berry, underlines the urgency of this attentiveness in the community of life:

> We should be clear about what happens when we destroy the living forms of this planet. The first consequence is that we destroy modes of divine presence. If we have a wonderful sense of the divine, it is because we live amid such awesome magnificence. If we have refinement of emotion and sensitivity, it is because of the delicacy, the fragrance, and indescribable beauty of song and music and rhythmic movement in the world about us. If we grow in our life vigor, it is because the earthly community challenges us, forces us to struggle and survive, but in the end reveals itself as benign providence.[14]

We may want to ask ourselves what sort of transformation process is required in order to realise that the silencing of any life or voice is tantamount to silencing the divine. Our social institutions and religious traditions have tended to reinforce the estrangement of the human from all other life forms. I believe that the shift we are being asked to make, enabling us to consider ourselves rooted in the primary community of all life, is like a growing or maturing in our humanity. History shows us how women, slaves, etc. have been viewed as objects rather than subjects, a worldview which is slowly changing. Perhaps as we grow more in our humanity as the conscious self-reflective ability of the universe, we will be able to broaden our concept of subject from that which appears to look like us to embrace all beings in the sacred community, which is the universe. Only then will subjectivity become real.

## Interconnectedness – The Dancers and the Dance

Who am I without the Sun, the elements and stars from which I was born? Where would the primrose be without the seed, soil, water and flower community that nurtured it? How would the universe be without the atoms, stars, galaxies, planets, rocks, bacteria, insects, plants, flowers, animals, birds and humans who sing its melodies to the winds, waves and deepest recesses of space? The third tendency of the universe is toward communion with itself. No being exists in the universe except in the community of the whole. The universe is one, a communion with itself in all its manifestations. To be is to be in communion, to be in relationship. Existence apart from community is an ontological impossibility. Human beings are not homogenous; everything that exists is kin, is bound in essence to everything else, is one. John Muir, Scottish-American naturalist, captured this reality when he wrote: 'When you try to take out anything by itself, you find it hitched to everything else in the universe'.

The primary bonding in the physical order is by means of gravitational attraction. The gift of gravity is amazing. Life is in a spin with planet Earth journeying round the Sun and rotating on its own axis at the same time yet the community of life is not hurtled off into the depths of space. In fact Earth holds us so securely that we think of ourselves as scarcely moving at all. I recall the feeling from my first plane journey many years ago. I was amazed at being able to enjoy a meal with no spills while flying at an altitude of over thirty-three thousand feet. The unifying force of gravity in the evolution of the universe can be seen as a model for the interconnectedness of the entire community of life. We think of human affection, but do we realise that the very attraction that holds the stars together in their orbit is what draws us in bonding with one another?

I think of the energy we expend in inter-human relationships almost to the exclusion of all other beings. What about the trees, the night sky, the insects, birds, animals and plants; do these have need of company? We belong together, all emanating from stardust and breathing the same air that is constantly recycling its way around the planet and across the ages. In uprooting the rainforests, polluting the air, soil, water, in alienating ourselves from other beings in the community of life, we are in fact maiming or destroying our own body. We are being challenged into holding the mirror of a communing universe up to our selfish behaviour, of overcoming the schizophrenic stance of being connected yet acting as if separate. In our sacred depths, each of us yearns to be recognised, nurtured and loved, to be in communion with all. Our desire for intimacy, for relationship, is at the heart of the universe.

## Framework for a Global Ethic

I imagine the three guiding principles of the universe as a prism reflecting light, sparkle, colour and direction on our journey into the future as the community of all creation. The words of Ivone Gebara, feminist theologian and social activist, speaking of the Christian Trinity, spring to mind: 'universal breathing together', which I see as the living communion of all beings. Andrei Rublev, early fifteenth-century Russian artist, inspired by Genesis 18 created a wonderful picture of the Triune God. Here Sarah and

Abraham welcome three strangers to their home and share hospitality with them, likewise the image of the Trinity with open space is welcome for all. What difference might the three principles of diversity, interiority and interconnectedness make in terms of our present anthropocentric way of being and acting? I think of the 'major surgery' required by our existing systems – social, political, economic and religious. Where would gender inequality, economic inequality, species inequality and the foundation stories of our major religious traditions fit in light of these values?

### Earth-Wise
In the earlier days of space exploration some astronauts shared their experience of seeing planet Earth from space. With their first glance back they immediately scanned for their home town. Then, with widening focus, they began to pick up specific features of their country's landscape. Only then could they suddenly see planet Earth in its wholeness. We too are being nudged to widen our horizons, to deepen our consciousness of the entire universe as one gigantic system. All other systems, for example, the galactic system, solar system and earth system are sub-systems of the overarching universe system. A system, or 'holon' (Greek holos, whole), is more than the sum of the parts, the relationship between the parts is also important. A system is both a 'whole' and a part; for example, a cell is whole in itself but also part of an organ, which is part of a living being. Planet earth is a 'whole' and part of a greater 'whole' – the universe.

Earth emerged within the Solar system about 4.5 billion years ago. It is a sub-system of the Universe. It self-regulates, self-organises and self-maintains. When one looks more closely at the functioning of Earth one becomes awed at the dynamics of the Earth system, the living Gaia. Thomas Berry identifies these core activities of the Earth: self-emergent, self-propagating, self-nourishing, self-educating, self-governing, self-healing and self-fulfilling. As we examine these let's try to imagine what life might be like if we were to align our humanly constructed systems with the systems of Earth. In doing this we will get a glimpse of how far we have strayed from intimacy with the Earth and, more importantly, how much richer our lives would be if we recognised and valued our place in the community of all life.

We will begin by pausing for a moment: every instant more than a million new faces emerge from the creativity of the Earth and Sun. How amazing! In our deepest core we can proclaim with delight that 'we are one in a million'. The cloud, dandelion, spider, blade of grass and cow are similarly unique. Each being in the human and natural world is unique and has the basic right to habitat, food, the nurturing of their young and the opportunity to realise their full potential within the total community of creation.

The challenge facing humans, mindful of our immersion in the total community, is to join the Earth community as a participating member. This means that we endeavour to create physical structures that will complement, not contradict, the physical workings of the entire Earth community. Our housing and transport (with the sheer amount of resources involved) can have devastating effects on the community of life, particularly in habitat destruction. This is counter to the self-emergent abilities of the planet. We, particularly in the western world, have become so dependent on fossil fuels and petroleum based products, for example, plastics and synthetic fabrics like rayon, nylon and polyester. The world is currently living (and growing) by drawing on its "savings account" of energy (sunlight) stored in fossil fuels (oil, coal, gas).'[15] It is urgent that we accelerate the production of alternative energies: solar, hydro, wind, wave and plant-based. According to the WorldWatch Institute 2003, renewable technologies have improved significantly: 'Global clean energy markets exceeded $10 billion in 2001 and are expected to surpass $82 billion by 2010.' However, there is a long way to go and the journey is made all the more difficult when mega-consumers like the United States, Canada and Australia remain defiant while others that pledge support fail to live up to their word, including, on occasion, our own country. This is further complicated when our actions in terms of the environment are motivated for the benefit of humanity alone rather than from the perspective of the total life community. The evolutionary story of the Universe leaves us in no doubt about our *oneness*, it is so critical that we allow this to shape our lives, our attitudes, values and priorities.

The Earth is self-nourishing and self-healing through the miracle of photosynthesis (nourishment) and its powers of regeneration (healing). Members of the community of Earth nourish each other in the established patterns of the natural world for the well being of all. There are the teeming oceans, the seeds of plants and trees, the pollen in flowers, the fertility of the soil and above all the Sun, source of all life on Earth. We become aware of the re-generative powers of Earth, for example, after periods of drought or forest fires. We witness this miracle in our own bodies, for example, how cuts and gashes heal and injuries disappear in time through the bodies' healing properties. We can assist these nourishing and healing properties by stopping the flow of toxins, pesticides and harmful chemicals into the Earth, by being attuned to the rhythms and energy patterns in our own bodies and valuing rest and fallow space. The process is helped in composting organic material, saving seeds, growing organic produce, shopping ethically and managing our waste. Above all, this requires a change of attitude and behaviour.

We live amid an abundance of resources, many of which are nonetheless finite. How might we use them in a more sustainable way?[16] I like to illustrate this choice by taking the example of a buffet supper. Most of us are familiar with the dynamic – tables of delicious food are laid, there is more than enough for everyone – but if you happen to be in the last third of the queue your luck invariably runs out especially for those mouth-watering egg and onion sandwiches or vol-au-vents. One would almost be inclined to blame the hosts for the shortage of food until the left-overs are gathered, some even untouched. This mirrors the behaviour of many of us with regard to our daily use of the resources of the planet. Richard Douthwaite in his book *The Growth Illusion*, describes a sustainable world economy:

> It would be localized rather than globalized. It would have no net capital flows. Its external trade would be confined to unimportant luxuries rather than essentials. Each self-reliant region would develop to a certain point and then stop rather than grow continuously. Investment decisions would be made close to home. And assets would be owned by the people of the area in which they are located.[17]

Those of us who are over-extractive in our use of Earth's bounty operate, I believe, out of a vision of scarcity rather than abundance. Planet earth is endowed with rich reserves of natural capital. What might appear to be greed is very often a sense of inferiority or fear of being bereft hence the need to grab and hoard. Therefore the making of money becomes the goal with all else, including the quality of life for all species, rendered incidental. This runs far deeper than economics; it is a power struggle for supremacy. Somehow people are driven by a compulsion to subdue the Earth, to tame, redesign and control the world of nature. This has led to the dangerous illusion that our advancing technologies can transcend the limits of nature. It is urgent that those who care about living in partnership with the natural world continue to work passionately to ensure that the abundant natural capital reserves, now under severe threat in many areas, are preserved into the future for the sake of the entire community of life:

> To restore healthy economic and social function, we must create economic institutions that restore money to its proper role as a facilitator of livelihood creation. This means transforming societies driven by the love of money into societies dedicated to the love of life.[18]

In our contemporary world, particularly in the western mind, there is a growing emphasis on self-fulfilment with psychologists and humanistic thinkers alike stressing that this is the goal of human purposeful behaviour. My question is: 'can self-fulfilment be legitimately achieved by some at the expense of others in the human community or by humans apart from the self-fulfilment of the community of life, which is the universe?' Thomas Berry is categorical in response:

> We cannot discover ourselves without first discovering the universe, the earth, and the imperatives of our own being. Each of these has a creative power and a vision far beyond any rational thought or cultural creation of which we are capable. Nor should we think of these as isolated from our own individual being or from the human community. We have no existence except within the earth and within the universe.[19]

When we consider the pollution of planet Earth, the devastation of precious natural resources, does it ever occur to us that this is a mirror image of an inner psychic disarray? When we say that some thing doesn't cost the earth, will we realise that this takes on a whole new meaning from the perspective of the community of all life? Cost is much more than monetary worth. The cost of living as we know it presently in the Euro Zone, while high and rising, is so much more when we take the entire community of life into consideration. I believe that it is only when we begin to think like this and weigh up the real cost that conversion begins to happen. Perhaps, it is a question of asking if we really *need* a particular commodity or if we simply *want* it?

The self-governing tendency of Earth is primarily manifested in the fundamental right of every species to habitat, nourishment and the opportunity to grow to their full potential. There are the changing seasons, the hydrological cycle, the ebb and flow of the tides, climate and weather patterns, the salinity of the oceans, pollinating plants, the meticulous building of topsoil, the living patterns of coral reefs and forest communities, all involved in the economy of Earth. Supposing we were to try and quantify in monetary terms some of the above self-governing services of Earth that nourish and sustain life in all its forms, what would the mathematics look like? In terms of governance where does militarism fit? In 2001 (most recent year for which data are available), the Stockholm International Peace Research Institute estimated world military expenditures at $839 billion. This amounts to $2.3 billion each day or almost $100 million an hour.[20] This is a conservative estimate and does not include the Iraq War and subsequent violence and devastation in terms of human life and contamination of the environment on which all life depends. We will assist the earth in self-governance to the extent that we integrate our systems of governance with those of the natural world. This means working to make warfare, whether over land, water, oil or whatever, a historical artefact, while living and working out of a consciousness of the well-being of the entire community of creation.

The self-educating of Earth manifests itself through physical, biological, chemical and cultural patterning. The basis of the education process is learning the story. The entire evolutionary process is a most remarkable feat of self-education, the billions of experiments in designing the existing life system. The wisdom of the three guiding principles of diversity, interiority and interconnectedness describe the self-educating process of earth. The story of the absolute oneness of all life is critical in enabling humans to move from their isolation and embrace the 'sacred hoop', the miraculous web of life. Children need to learn from the natural world, the Book of Nature, as well as from human techniques and it is crucial that we lead them to see themselves as members of the whole community of life not just of the human global community.

Our education system, confined almost exclusively to the classroom and laboratory, is limited in terms of helping us reconnect more deeply with the Earth, our primary teacher, and living as members of the total life community. How much more exciting it would be for our children to be involved directly with the soil, to learn gardening and the value of food, to understand the energy of the Sun and other sources of alternative energy, to learn the beauty, power and carrying capacity of their bioregion and, above all, to find their rightful place in the community of creation. This broader context would serve as a basis for the curriculum – science, humanities, religion, economics, geography, mathematics, the arts and so forth.

We can take heart from the various signs of the human and natural world in global partnership. There are the efforts of countless individuals, families and local communities working for a better quality of life for all species. There is the growing number of Earth literacy initiatives worldwide and more recently in Ireland, for example, An Gairdín, (Co. Galway), Roscarbery (Co. Cork), An Tairseacht (Co. Wicklow), Brú na Cruinne, (Co. Tipperary) and a number of emerging ones where the new story of the Universe is the context and the renewal of the Earth the vision that shapes the future. The creation of a part time masters degree in *Ecology & Religion* by The Columban Missionaries (Dalgan Park, Navan) and the University of Wales Lampeter in 2002 is key in the education process. The Organic Centre (Co. Leitrim), Sonairte (Co. Meath), Dollinger (Co. Limerick), Ballymaloo Cookery Centre (Cork), Voice (Dublin), Cultivate, Sustainable Living Centre (Dublin), Friends of the Earth (Dublin & UK), Sustainable Northern Ireland Programme (Belfast) ECOS Centre (Ballymena), Castle Espie, Oxford Island and Armagh

Planetarium (N. Ireland) together with Klee Paper Products (Dublin & Cork), Repak, recycling packaging waste, BirdWatch Ireland, Crann: Releafing Ireland, The Irish Peatland Conservation Council, Astronomy Ireland, Seedsavers Association of Ireland and Irish Organic Farmers and Growers Association, are some notable examples of commitment to consciousness raising and education in sustainable living.

Ireland still lags behind many other European countries in terms of commitment to sustainable living. It is heartening, however, to see the spread of Local Council recycling centres and governmental initiatives at this time of enormous stress on the environment, for example, the plastic bag tax and smoking ban in pubs and restaurants. It is interesting to note how a small country like Ireland could be transformed virtually overnight from using an estimated one and a quarter billion plastic bags per annum, the majority of which littered our hedgerows and countryside leaching into the soil, water and air, to a nation substantially free of plastic bags. Government initiatives, for example, ENFO, information on the Environment, Environment Protection Agency, Forest Stewardship Council, An Taisce and Green Schools are important in the ongoing education process. A greater commitment is needed, particularly at political level, with other parties consolidating the pioneering role of the Green Party.

The Earth is self-fulfilled in each of its components, in the evolving story of the universe – the twinkling of the stars, music of the waters, the flowering of plants, trees and flowers, the flight of birds, the hum of insects, in the changing seasons and the patient work of microbes. We participate in this self-fulfilling function as the Earth reflecting on itself in self-awareness. This will become a reality through learning the story, our cosmological heritage, and envisioning a future full of hope which we shape and celebrate in ritual, music, dance, poetry, drama, literature, technology, art and architecture.

With all the above mentioned efforts, and these are only some examples of the great work being done by millions of people, I have this vision of hope for the future if we were to re-imagine our initiatives and actions out of the context of the evolutionary story of the Universe. Planet Earth would be recognised as a network of interdependent communities forming the all-embracing community of life. The well-being of the human would be transformed into the well-being of all in the community of creation. What a transformation? What energy and vitality we would share in coming home to our rightful place in the community of life.

A key way of making this vision a reality is by entering into one's bioregion. This means acknowledging that a particular area or region is much more than the total human population and its technologies and systems, however advanced and influential. Then, and only then, will we be able to encounter the magnificent community of other life forms characterising the bioregion. There are the ancient rocks, elements, waterways and soil, climate and weather conditions, the flora and fauna combining with human presence in lilting our common bioregional tune. My belief is that we will wake up to our sense of belonging in the community of all creation primarily through interacting as the human community with other beings in the natural world.

I was enjoying being cradled by the soft, green grass as I listened to the familiar tune of the Atlantic waves creeping up behind me, stealthily. This is Culdaff, my home beach, the faithful carrier of so many of my joys, sorrows, questions, hopes, dreams and trusted friends on life's journey. The tiny wild flowers colouring my bed were bewitching me, drawing me into the silence of mystery...

*and as I listened I could faintly hear*
*the heart beat of billions of creatures, echoes of the divine,*
*over billions of years in tune with mine*
*drawing closer, closer, like violin music straining in crescendo*
*edging higher and higher.*
*My heart quickened in awe, overwhelmed*
*Where have I been until now?*
*Shall I miss this moment too, all billions of years of it?*
*Perchance, I'll wake outright to witness*
*solid rock masses extend soft, wide arms*
*in communion invitation to our multi-specied neighbourhood*
*and behold with ever-widening eyes, blinking in disbelief,*
*all manner of creature emerge*
*from tombs of alienation — silenced and solidified — in human hearts*
*slowly, reverently, embracing and joyfully proclaiming WE ARE ONE!*
*Hereafter, shall I nestle more securely in the lap of Mother Earth, as of*
*old intuitively,*
*now with the universe intimate way of knowing, heart beat to heart beat.*

## Notes

1. Reported in *News of the World*, 8 February 2004, 42-43
2. *The Dream of the Earth* Thomas Berry, Introduction xiii, (Sierra Club Books, San Francisco, 1988). Berry heralds the dawning of a new age of mutually enhancing human-earth relationships and speaks of moving beyond democracy to biocracy in which the larger community of life will participate in our human decision-making processes. He cites the World Charter for Nature passed by the United Nations Assembly in 1982.

3. Sisyphus was a character in Greek mythology. His punishment was to roll a huge stone to the top of a hill. He had to do this with his nose and with every advance the stone kept rolling back again.
4. *Introduction to Systems Philosophy – Towards a New Paradigm of Contemporary Thought* Ervin Laszlo (Gordon & Breach, New York, 1984).
5. *Building The Earth* Teilhard de Chardin 37 Geoffrey Chapman London Dublin 1965
6. *The Phenomenon of Man* Teilhard de Chardin, 63, (Harper & Row, New York, London, San Francisco, 1955).
7. General information from *Putting Life Before Debt* 8 (Caritas International, Rome, CIDSE, Belgium, 1998). This text is a view of international debt from the perspective of Catholic social teaching as it looked towards the year of Jubilee and debt reduction or obliteration.
8. Reported in *Resurgence*, 14, May/June 2001 (Business Ethics quote)
9. Reported in *The Ecologist*, 13 September 2002 (Advert placed in *Fortune* magazine by the Philippine government).
10. *The Dream of the Earth* Thomas Berry, 195, (Sierra Club Books, San Francisco, 1988).
11. 'Any Tree Will Listen' by Shelby Allen published in *EarthLight Magazine* Spring 2002 Issue 45 Vol. 12 No.3 Oakland, CA.
12. *Summa Theologica* Thomas Aquinas, Part One, Question 47, Article One.
13. *The Power of Now* Eckhart Tolle, 65, (Hodder & Stoughton, 1999).
14. *The Dream of the Earth* Thomas Berry, 11, (Sierra Club Books, San Francisco, 1988).
15. *The Last Hours of Ancient Sunlight* Thom Hartmann, 26, (Three Rivers Press, New York, 1998).
16. In 1987, the World Commission on Environment and Development in its Report *Our Common Future* (The Brundtland Report), defined sustainable development as 'that which meets the needs of the present without compromising the ability of future generations to meet their own needs'. This echoes the Native American philosophy that we must think of seven generations hence in terms of using Mother Earth's precious gifts.
17. *The Growth Illusion* Richard Douthwaite, 344, (Green Books, UK 1992, 1999).

Respect

18. Ibid. (Foreword xiii by David C. Korten).
19. *The Dream of The Earth* Thomas Berry, 195, (Sierra Club Books, San Francisco, 1988).Berry believes that 'even beyond the earth, we need to go to the universe and inquire concerning the basic issues of reality and value, for, even more than the earth, the universe carries the deep mysteries of our existence within itself'.
20. Reported in *Vital Signs 2003 Military Expenditure on the Rise 118* The WorldWatch Institute (W.H. Norton, New York, London, 2003).

# FURTHER READING

Berry, Thomas 1988, *The Dream of the Earth*, Sierra Club Books, San Francisco.

Berry Thomas, 1998, *The Great Work*, Bell Tower Publications New York.

Conlon, James 1994, *Earth Story, Sacred Story*, Twenty-Third Publications Mystic CT.

Conrow Coelho, Mary 2002, *Awarening Universe, Emerging Personhood*, Wyndham Hall press, USA.

Cotgreave, Peter & Irwin Forseth 2002, *Introductory Ecology*, Blackwell Science Ltd USA, UK.

Dames, Michael, 1992, *Mythic Ireland*, Thames and Hudson London.

Douthwaite, Richard, 1999, *The Growth Illusion*, Green Books, Ltd UK.

Fabel, Arthur & Donald St. John eds, 2003, *Teilhard in the 21st Century*, Orbis Books.

Fallon, Sally, 1995, *Nourishing Traditions*, ProMotion Publishing, CA.

Hartmann, Thom, 1998, 1999, *The Last Hours of Ancient Sunlight*, Three Rivers Press, New York, New York.

# Further Reading

Hayden, Tom, 1996, *The Lost Gospel of the Earth*, Sierra Book Club, San Francisco.

Kumar, Satish, 2002, *You Are Therefore I Am*, Green Books Ltd, UK.

Lovelock, James, 1979, *Gaia: A New Look at Life on Earth*, Oxford University Press.

Macy, Johanna & Molly Young Brown, 1998, *Coming Back to Life*, New Society, Canada.

Mc Donagh, Sean, 2001, *Why Are We Deaf to the Cry of the Earth?*, Veritas, Dublin.

McDonagh, Sean, 2004, *Dying For Water*, Veritas, Dublin.

McFague, Sallie, 1993, *The Body of God: An Ecological Theology*, Fortress Press, MS.

O'Murchu, Diarmuid, 1997, *Quantum Theology*, The Crossroads Publishing Company, New York.

Porritt, Jonathan, 2000, *Playing Safe: Science and the Environment*, Thames & Hudson, UK.

Primavesi, Anne, 2000, *Sacred Gaia*, Rutledge, London New York.

Tucker, Mary E. & J.A. Grim, eds., 1994, *Worldviews and Ecology*, Orbis Books, Maryknoll, New York.

Shiva, Vandana, 2000, *Stolen Harvest*, South End Press, Cambridge, MA.

Swimme, Brian, 1996, *The Hidden Heart of the Cosmos*, Orbis Books, Maryknoll, NY.

Swimme & Thomas Berry eds., *The Universe Story*, Harper San Francisco.

The Organic Centre, Rossinver, Co. Leitrim, 2003, *A Guide to Home Composting*.

Uhl, Christopher, 2004, *Developing Ecological Consciousness*, Rowman & Littlefield Publishers, Inc. USA.

Wackernagel, Mathis & William Rees, 1996, *Our Ecological Footprint*, New Society Publishers, Canada.

Ward, Peter & Donald Brownlee, 1999, *Rare Earth*, Springer-Verlag Telos, New York.

Wilson, Edward O., 1992, 2001, *The Diversity of Life*, Penguin Books, New York, London, Toronto.

Wilson, Edward O., 2002, *The Future of Life*, A Little, Brown Book, Great Britain.